THE MYSTERY OF LAWLESSNESS

The Final Dimension

PASTOR KEYWORTH N. NGOSA

iUniverse, Inc.
New York   Bloomington

THE MYSTERY OF LAWLESSNESS
The Final Dimension

iUniverse books may be ordered through booksellers or by contacting:

iUniverse
1663 Liberty Drive
Bloomington, IN 47403
www.iuniverse.com
1-800-Authors (1-800-288-4677)

ISBN: 978-1-4502-0885-7 (pbk)
ISBN: 978-1-4502-0886-4 (ebk)

Printed in the United States of America

iUniverse rev. date: 02/26/2010

To
Keyworth N. Ngosa Jnr
My Brother, My Friend and My Son
We have a challenge before us and the best
We could ever do is to be informed, transformed and be Reformers.
The world needs our resolve or else it will perish
And us with it

Contents

Acknowledgements

T*o the countless people that have been there for me at every moment in life I salute you. It's not always easy to single out individuals when so many have played a vital role. Some of you we only met for a few minutes, but those few minutes you changed my life.*

H*onor in its totality can only come from God. To you who have played that significant role, no matter how small it may have appeared, surely honor awaits you.*

A*nd what better way of investment could be compared to eternal bliss… When that day dawns and dawn it shall, you will be crowned and move majestically in royal regalia on the golden boulevards of Heaven.*

N*umbers too large to be computed by human imagination will clap for you. They will echo your names. Every life of God that you help, every child of the Most High that you extend your warm heart to will be your blessing.*

K*eep up the good work. Do not relent. Do not stop with me. Don't limit your blessing. You will drink of the river of His pleasures. How sweet it is to know there is pleasure, abundant and undefiled pleasure in Him our Lord, The Great I AM.*

S*urely your resolve to support His work has paid off. In your hands is your hope, your faith and love towards Him materialized. There can be no greater joy than knowing you have touched lives many of whom you will only meet in the next life.* Thanks.

Introduction

I*t is heart rending to realize the subject before us is the greatest downfall of many. No sensible person would find it a joy when a soul is lost eternally. It is my sincere desire that many people's eyes will be opened to what lies before us. I was awestruck the time the Lord showed me the real mark of the Beast.*

N*ever in my wildest imagination had I realized it was this close. Never had I known the mark is already on display and people are going for it. And many never to return.*

T*he insight God has given me to understand the Three Kingdoms: The Kingdom of God, The Kingdom of Man and The Kingdom of Satan, I put them down for you to see. How I pray that you grasp the issue at hand. Things are not as they really seem to be.*

R*easons are being given for the state of the world by various people, but the truth of the matter is that the real reasons are not being divulged. In fact they are keeping them under lock and key. The Bible clearly states that before the Lord Jesus comes back, two things will happen—many Christians will fall away, they will backslide and the man of sin the Antichrist will be revealed.*

O*ur undivided resolve is the key to help us escape the various schemes that are being implemented. There are a lot of things that are beyond ordinary eyes and ears; now you have the opportunity to see things as they are. The devil is fooling people about the extent of his wickedness, while he prepares his own to take over the world. We cannot afford to slumber. Not even for a second.*

Keyworth N. Ngosa

I. Creating The Atmosphere

2 Thessalonians 2:7 *'for the mystery of lawlessness is already at work...'*

A. Failing Political System 1

Isaiah 13:7 *Therefore shall all hands be faint,*
and every man's heart
shall melt

Frustration, failure and confusion are staring the world in the face, and the world does not know what to do. Total chaos is imminent. Dejection is greeting the masses every day. Everywhere you go people seem to be facing hopelessness. They can just put their undying faith and hope in the political system. This is their all. If only a great and wise leader could emerge, then all would be like the good old days. People have time and again put all their trust and hope in the political leaders they elect. They hope for a good today and a better tomorrow. But what confuses them is how a promising leader just fails to fulfill or deliver his or her promises.

All of a sudden a leader who was a lamb becomes a monster, he or she begins to bellow. Dictatorial tendencies become a lifestyle. *What happened to the sweet person they elected?* **The best definition of a leader that every person on the streets understands is one who sacrifices himself for the sake of the people.** Today it is one who sacrifices the people for his sake! Good conditions for politicians and poor conditions for the masses. The poor get poorer and the rich richer. Everyone has his share. It all depends on the position you occupy on the food chain. You are either the predator or the prey.

It is undeniable that the ugly face of hunger that is already confronting us will surely intensify. The statistics are giving us figures we all wish were just a bad dream and not the ugly reality right before us. Almost 20% of the world population is grappling for a loaf of bread, which when they find, they will just sniff at and their eyes roll up and more souls are lost, never to come back. Calls for the G 8 to do something have been coming and going. **To no avail. It seems the black horse of scarcity in the Book of Revelation has come sooner than anticipated.** World catastrophes are imminent: tsunamis wiping thousands of people in a few hours, and leaving more in an incomprehensible struggle for survival, hurricanes; Katrina for example—hitting New Orleans and leaving it rubble. One would think such pain is a third world countries' affair. That is not reality. People who once had it all, in minutes become homeless and devastated. Inexplicable perennial fires that consume people's livelihood and hopes, the unrelenting droughts that lick up lives of infants and adults without any discrimination, squeezing life out of a person in the most painful manner—starvation. Earthquakes that wipeout thousands in a few hours. Truly the world is living on the very cusp of the fangs of death. Terrorism— something that is now hard to define, is rife. Terrorism today is defined by the side you are on, for even the so-called terrorists think the fella on the other side of the street is the terrorist.

Let us not forget September 11, it's etched on our hearts, it left thousands of souls dead and transformed the security of the entire world. Indirectly or is it directly, the ensuing war on terror has claimed a lot more souls than the almost 3000 who perished that day. September 11 has claimed more lives than we shall ever know—Iraqi war for example, is one such result of that fateful day. Suicide bombs being detonated everywhere. *Who is safe?* With the security of the world in jeopardy after terror attacks politicians are busy with policies to help the world. But some believe the policies are unstable and could lead to intense conflagration. The West lock horns with the Arab extremists. *Who is an extremist?* Hard to define. Is the world any safer?

It is regrettable, quite shameful, but unfortunately true that if you want to see civil wars you don't have to look far. Come to Africa. They are manufactured here at the slightest excuse. In Africa it is now a trend to think of negotiating when we run out of bullets. We are more determined to fight than to reason. As if that were not enough, strange diseases like bird flu, swine flu, Ebola—a disease that could finish a person in 24 hours—are rising! Global warming. The fear of radiation related diseases. Nobody is safe. Add to this mess, diseases like AIDS, and you have the final ingredient to this witches' brew. *The world just got ugly.*

No wonder the masses are screaming, it is heart melting. What is the world coming to? Masses flee to the politicians for help as they cry; **help**. Help; use the taxpayers' money to help us. Alas .The government drags its feet and shrugs its shoulders. That could only mean one thing. An omen. **'There ain't no money!'** *How could it be?!* The masses roar in disbelief. For sure how could it be, their mere pittance of incomes are viciously taxed and over taxed. For what? For such eventualities, but when they come and come they do, lo and behold there is no money. A responsible parent looks at the waxen faces of his family members and sees death extending its tentacles towards them. He cannot allow this to happen. He cannot bury his family, not without a fight. Tempers swell and flare. Riots erupt. The people riot and the police move in to quell the disturbance. Protests and threats come to a colossal collision. Trained police *mistakenly* fire live ammunition. It is chaos. Confusion everywhere.

Governments become unpopular, shame covers the leadership. Finger pointing begins and scapegoats are made out of the innocent. Mr. President has no other choice but to step down. No one will take his well–oiled explanation. He cannot even lick his wounds; his tongue is too dry to do that. Speechless, he cannot understand the way the world economies are plunging to disaster. The sweet–tongued opposition leaders step on the podium, promising nothing less than gold and diamond for every citizen. Eyes bulge with expectation. Saliva drips from people's eyes, ears, nostrils and mouths. Salvation has come. Halleluiah.

People however, realize in a trice they have been had. This genius is no genius at all. The cycle begins. People begin to refer to the previous leader as having been better. It is not scientific knowledge to note that the only people eager to vote are those in power and those who are trying to get in power. The rest? They are showing lack of confidence in voting generally. For them to vote they need incentives and there are only two incentives at the moment—pay them or send soldiers to poke them to vote (Maybe even the soldiers themselves need some incentives). Friend, it seems people have not seen anything worth voting for, so they have gone on a global voting protest. This is the global situation at the moment. And this 'moment' has lasted a life time, in many areas.

One could look at things from another angle and say today people are abnormally impatient, individually and collectively. They cannot wait for anything that is not instant. The virtue of waiting went through the window a long time ago. So, it is not the leadership that is a problem, but the impatient masses. They want instant this, they want instant that. In the end, we see proliferation of drug victims, sexual victims, fatal business deals, gambling victims, rise in satanic practices to get instant success, the list goes on and on. It is a vicious cycle. The masses maintain the leadership is bad.

Leaders today are rarely appreciated. Nowadays there are only two great leaders. A former one. And a dead one. People, do not speak good of a current leader. *Make your own finding.* It does not matter the nation. It is all the same. And with such intense yearning for solace, the world or masses cry for quicker and faster solutions. *Whoever has a solution for this problem had better bring it fast. As soon as yesterday.*

It is imperative to note that when a person is desperate, he loses the sense of direction. Instinct replaces reason. Survival steps in. The masses wanted to make Jesus their king by force. Meaning whatever king they had was going to be deposed and Jesus enthroned. For what reason? He could provide better bacon. John 6:15. They never cared whether Jesus was holy or not as long as He could provide food, they were happy. Empty stomachs have caused many regrettable decisions in the past, the consequences of which we live with. Child of God, what the masses today do not know, what is hidden from their eyes is the power behind all this suffering.

There is something beyond ordinary eyes and ears. A language. A language hidden from the ears of the masses. An understanding that can only be comprehended when you are at a certain frequency. May the Holy Spirit open your eyes and ears so that you fully grasp within you what lies before us. The Bible says Satan is the god of this world. 2 Cor.

4:4. What does that mean? Doesn't the same Bible say God created this world Gen. 1:1, Psalm 24:1, how come? Ok this is how come. Are you ready? God created this earth, but the system being used is the devil's.

In graphic terms we say the world is like computer hardware. God created it but, the 'world' the Bible is talking about in Corinthians is like the operating system—windows, Linux, apple... The hardware is God's but the operating system is Satan's. *Get the picture, Tom?*

Christians must know that the world which was designed by God is running on a system foreign to the designer. It is running on Satan's system. Satan has done all he could to convince the world that his operating system is the best and only system. This is the biggest problem we are facing today. This is the greatest cause of divisions among believers. Some Christians know what is going on, while others are snoring. And it is those who have been snoring who are the noisiest. *Everything is okay, everything is okay.* Wait a minute, on whose pay roll are you? Things are not okay. When there are cover–ups, spiritual covert operations, to enlist many into the devil's system, it can't be okay. The system is not okay. In the beginning God put Adam in charge of the earth, that is **The Original Rule**. But that rule was squashed when Adam lost his position to the devil in **The Overthrow**. The devil begun to rule. After the fall, God still reached out to man to give him the system by which the earth could be governed, this is **The Omega Rule.** Understand this very well. This is the key to everything in this book. In fact it is the key to understanding the events and issues today. So there is

- **The Original Rule: Adamic Rule**
- **The Overthrow: Satanic Rule**
- **The Omega Rule: Christ's Rule**

After Adam's fall, the devil did all he could to spread his reign on earth, for he had become the master. He did it in such a way that it would be appealing at first but the grand bitter finale could not be anticipated until it was too late for man to reverse. His main goal was to totally own man and the earth. The Omega Rule, the Rule of God was obliterated from the surface of the earth from its inception. The devil killed it in its infancy. God pointed out the desires of the people and how it would cost them, that is why He chose His own system, the Omega Rule. But they refused. *What does the Omega Rule say anyway?*

The King

Deuteronomy 17:14 *When you enter the land the* LORD *your God is giving you and have taken possession of it and settled in it, and you say, "Let us set a king over us like all the nations around us,"*[15] *be sure to appoint over you the king the* LORD *your God chooses. He must be from among your own brothers. Do not place a foreigner over you, one who is not a brother Israelite.*

God told the people that when they started admiring the political systems of the nations that were not under Him, they were at least supposed to take a leader whom God had appointed. And the Lord did not keep it a secret, He could not entrust the rule of the world to any other person. He had someone in mind. **So, all the leaders who were to be chosen were just temporal or caretaker leaders. They were to hand over the throne of world governance to one person.** God wanted the system to flow that way. That is why God Himself was interested in who ascended to the throne. The Caretaker leaders had to be chosen by God Himself. He even laid down certain guide lines for all the leaders who would ascend to the throne. These leaders were not to surround themselves with the security of the unbelievers, but their shield had to be none but God, the decider of the outcome of any battle. **God totally forbade the adoption of foreign ways because He knew what lay behind them**. God forbade these caretakers from marrying many women because that would lead them astray.

A sexually immoral life destroys a leader. A leader of God's people was forbidden from acquiring a lot of money because that too distorts vision and one begins to forget the reason he is on the throne. His greatest asset on the throne was to be God's eternal Word, which he had to meditate upon day and night so that he does not lose the fear of

God and does as the Lord tells him. *A leader of God's people should never think he is better than anyone of the people he is leading, regardless their status in society.* A leader despite being firm had to be sympathetic not merciless. **A leader had to know that he was on the throne because a particular need was required. And he had to thrive to bring it to reality.** But these caretaker leaders would bring it all and lay the right to rule before the only and awesome one, Jesus the Messiah.

Genesis 49:10 *The scepter or leadership shall not depart from Judah, nor the ruler's staff from between his feet, until Shiloh [the Messiah, the Peaceful One] comes to Whom it belongs, and to Him shall be the obedience of the people.(Amp)*

Genesis 49:10 *The scepter will not depart from Judah, nor the ruler's staff from between his feet, until he comes to whom it belongs and the obedience of the nations is his. (NIV)*

World rule belongs to Jesus, the last Adam. God had Jesus in mind to rule all the world. As King. But the devil has also been thinking. He has not accepted Isaiah 9:6. Satan has refused the Government to be upon Jesus' shoulders. The devil's idea is to make the world bow be fore his child, not God's child. He designed a system that has to lay the rule of the world at the feet of his child. The devil has totally refused God's system to be implemented. He has introduced his own.

Look at the scripture above, it uses the words **'be sure'** your king is chosen by God. But what have we decided to do like the great think tanks we are? Expel God unceremoniously.

1Samuel 8:7 *And the* LORD *told him: "Listen to all that the people are saying to you; it is not you they have rejected, but they have rejected me as their king.*

The people did not want to waste time. They gave God marching orders. Red card. Even His system was given marching orders. The devil was laughing, his plan was ripening. The Overthrow System was being implemented. God knew that the people would soon start appointing kings or presidents as they saw fit not as He intended. God's Omega Rule was a spiritual monarch. When God warned them, they said, *'Thank you for advising us, but we maintain, get out of our lives. And next time keep your advice to yourself!'* So it all started with worldly monarchs (not divine) and ended up in democracy! Just like that Democracy was born. Hooray. But God was quick to point out the dangers of the new system they were opting for. He did not hide the repercussions of democracy. Democracy friend was birthed out of the rejection of Theocracy. *I know am stepping on people's toes.* Democracy is their salvation. What does God say about democracy? Let's look at 1 Samuel 8 quickly.

1Samuel 8:11 *And he said, This will be the manner of the king that shall reign over you: He will take your sons, and appoint them for himself, for his chariots, and to be his horsemen; and some shall run before his chariots.*

God told them that in democracies their children would become the President's body guards, aides, advance party, secret service etc. All would revolve on his interests, not theirs. *Did they believe Him?* They thought He was bluffing. They laughed at Him, a desperate God they took Him to have been.

1Samuel 8:12 *And he will appoint him captains over thousands, and captains over fifties; and will set them to ear his ground, and to reap his harvest, and to make his instruments of war, and instruments of his chariots.*

God told them economically how dearly they would pay. The military would be for his safety and would be at his disposal. He would spend a lot on military, but that military would not be for your sake it would be for his sake mostly! Your wealth will be to make military equipment. He would send your children to war for his influence to grow. He would be very comfortable while hunger is leaking your shriveled stomachs because your children will sacrifice their own lives for his pleasure!

> 1Samuel 8:13 *And he will take your daughters to be confectionaries, and to be cooks, and to be bakers.*

'Your daughters would become his maids, dressers etc ,' God told them. Is this the case in Democracy?

> 1Samuel 8:14 *And he will take your fields, and your vineyards, and your oliveyards, even the best of them, and give them to his servants.*

Fasten your belts. Fasten your belts. Tighter. Tighter. But alas the people do not have even the belts to start with. Your interests will not be priority because those looking after him, he will give the best of the GDP. Are we seeing the raw deal? God is just telling us, '*I hate to say this, but I told you so.*' And He sure did.

> 1Samuel 8:15 *And he will take the tenth of your seed, and of your vineyards, and give to his officers, and to his servants.*

God told them that their democratically elected leader would tax them for the benefit of his attendants! From the word 'Go' nothing has been mentioned to benefit the people. Anyway let's wait and see. *Surely democracy can't fail us.* This is a well tested system, it works, it must work. But what is this we see? **There is nothing for the people.**

> 1Samuel 8:16 *And he will take your menservants, and your maidservants, and your goodliest young men, and your asses, and put them to his work.*

Everything is just about him? Whatever happened to the **'Government of the people by the people for the people?** All will be put to **'his'** work? Not the people's work? *Come on, God is a liar!!! God you are a liar. This can't be so. In Democracy we do not work for the Presidency, the Presidency works for us. Yeah. We hire and fire. Wow. Wonderful.*

> 1 Samuel 8:17 *He will take a tenth of your flocks, and you yourselves will become his slaves.*

When the people are overtaxed and have lost property at abnormal rates they will lose their freedom and become slaves. Look at this. *If this wasn't real life, this would definitely top the chart as the joke of the millennium.* Most of the people had just been told how their lives would improve if they 'sacrificed'. And sacrifice they did. Some genius told them all their woes would end if only they 'reached HIPC' completion point. HIPC became an issue. Property that made people independent and dignified was given at a mere pittance to satisfy HIPC conditions. People HIPC*ked.* And what followed? Oil woes. Oil reached *astronomical* prices; it was shooting towards $US200 a barrel. After the great debt cancellations, oil woes, insufficient energy and many such comical happenings ensued then the song of the millennium, the Credit Crunch. *After all the sacrifice the reward is the financial crunch?* And the genius just nods. The system is inhuman. **Raise their expectations but make them desperate. It is easier to make a slave out of a desperate fella.** Many who thought they were comfortable can't believe how the cruel tentacles of the system could easily pull them in to the vortex of confusion. No nation is spared. The devil is not a 'racist'. He attacks all with intense viciousness. And many are tottering on the edge of despair. They have come to their wits end. *'I hate to tell you this, but I told you so.'* I hear those words from God audibly. He designed His system to be lived using the Bible, but when we came up with the rule of the people by the people for the people he left it all to us. As we ejected the Bible from our lives we ejected our peace unknowingly. Desperation is hitting us hard now. Houses are being repossessed. **People are at the mercy of the political system.** Slavery is hitting us. High taxes, loved ones lost in unnecessary and very questionable wars, bread winners gone, companies plunging in the abyss out of the blues, why and how? Many are spiraling in debt more than before they HIPC*ked. You are going to see a deeper and worse debt crisis.* But whom does the world owe? Why can't we get out of this mess? Is it true we are in deeper waters than we were before HIPC tunes started playing? **Was the recession really unforeseen? Was it really mismanagement at high levels of 'bank management'?** Was it really lending without thinking? **Could competent bankers have suddenly lost their grey matter and just dished out money without second thoughts? Or is it one of the solutions to a nefarious scheme?** A scheme that has been there for years and years; *let them borrow themselves into slavery.* **A system closely guarded as it is passed on from one generation to the other to bring the whole world at the feet of the devil's son through national and individual debts?** A system that grinds the economy in only one direction. An inevitable system. A system only known and closely guarded by **a few global elite.** (*If only we knew that there are things beyond ordinary eyes and ears we wouldn't take life for granted). Enslave them* are the key words of this programme. Slaves?

Slaves to whom? Firstly to the president and the system, for the system they were choosing, is very enslaving. God warned them that a day would come when the people would cry for help. They argued with Him. Please take note Dave, that the system they were adopting was Universal. God told them He would not answer them when they really needed His help.

1 **S**amuel 8:18 *When that day comes, you will cry out*
for relief from the king you have chosen,
and the LORD *will not answer*
you in that day. "

To make the short story long, it has come upon us. What God warned has come to pass. Presidents are coming and going. It seems every president who comes with super approval ratings goes out in the fizzling life of disgrace. How could all presidents be bad? Don't they all want the best for their nations?

Yes, the best is what they want definitely. **A government of the people, by the people for the people**, a slogan, is all we have to show for, today. Everything else is disaster. **The Bible says there is no such a thing as a government of the people by the people for the**

people. That is another way of saying man is final, God get out. That unfortunately is the other face of humanism. In Luke 4 we see Satan coming to Jesus with three plans. He said to himself 'If *A doesn't work I will hit Jesus with B. If B doesn't work I will hit Him with C. And if C doesn't work, it's back to the drawing board*'. Democracy in its mature stage is a disaster to humanity. It is a sweet system in its infancy. But the devil knew that the greatest strength of democracy is its weakest point too. And that weak point would be unveiled in the last stages when the signal is given. Only the Omega Rule satisfies everyone and until then bloated tummies, riots, insults, wars, vote rigging and disputes, judicial unfairness, economic collapses etc will be as rare as salt water in the Indian Ocean... In real governance, the people's voice is not really heard. **Not all presidents are bad, it is the system.** The system dictates what ought to be done. The President in reality is not an individual. *You did not get it. I know you missed it. Presidents will come and go, but the system and the men behind the system remain.* That is what you must digest. The presidency is an establishment! **In the main, the people who control the presidency are not even in government.** They just have a few muppets here and there to oversee their interests. Until you know certain things, you will never know the pressures some presidents and governments go through. Someone is pulling them in another direction. **It is the size of those calling the shots that make some of our beloved leaders shrivel, like plants in the blazing and uncompromising Sahara orange ball.**

Serious understanding is needed here. The leadership will make clear unpopular decisions that will hurt the masses most of the times. The president has to bulldoze in most situations and not listen to the people who elected him into power, because the president is not a person, but a system. The presidency is a system, an organization and as we go global, we see that there must be a link. **For the system cannot ripen if it continues to operate as a cell.** It must unite. Regional groupings first then finally **One world Government with One Global Leader**. This is the second and ultimate step to slavery. This is the devil's definition or interpretation of Genesis 49:10. **Governments cannot continue operating like cells, they must become part of the global organism.** The great Kingdom of darkness of Revelation 12. This is the global solution the world is headed to. **This system has been in place**

for thousands of years. The devil has had this system in mind for a very long time and the times are ripe for it to be set. **The system the world rides on has been a well guarded secret in the higher places of wickedness.** Generations have been working on this for years and years. And the best part? We are fooled to look in the opposite direction when the implementers are next to us**. The whole idea of devil worship is to catch people unaware.** Man despite being a fallen creature can only go a certain level in accepting evil openly. So the devil has to work underground and release his poison slowly. That way fallen man will accept evil a bit by bit. Many people we drool before, many we howl and jump for are not as sweet as we think they are. They are the perpetrators of this insanity. And what gives them the courage is the amount of success they seem to have accomplished. The level of ignorance in the general populace, the plans that have gone well, the spheres of society they have pervaded, and the propagandas of their puppies who calm the masses telling them *such things don't exist*, when they, at the end of the day are to report to the **'same things which don't exist.'** The world must be ruled by an **elite Satanist!** This is where democracy is taking us, to be ruled by one person and it so happens, unfortunately, to be the devil's child. Our wisdom finally caught up with us. Let's clap for ourselves.

This kingdom, global kingdom is both physical and spiritual. And what better way of bringing the kingdom into global approval than through the economic slumps and trumped up fuel hocus-pocus, war and other related issues? **Listen, in all this confusion we are seeing, some people know what is really going on.** And others? They are just like chickens without heads. Flapping and fluttering all over the place. *You must have covered many levels to know certain secrets.* The devil is rowing us in the other direction. The good news is we are about to get a rude awakening. A rude awakening is not bad. At least we are awake. **Let me inform you that there is more than meets the eye.** The system has betrayed many presidents who have labored for the well being of the people. But once they work against the tide, they go out disgracefully. A lot of people do not give it a hoot whose system is in place as long as there is a system. But that is where the problem is. Never forget this next line Thelma. **Satan designed the world system to fail.** Looking at your face I know you didn't get it. Here is the replay. Satan designed the system in such a way that economies that are promising will collapse. *(I wrote this and have preached it years before the global economic meltdown. And by the way, what you just experienced is nothing compared to what is coming. In fact this was a simple test a flexing of the muscles to see if the system can malfunction at the pressing of a button. Sounds funny I know).* People will see their lives ebbing away right before their eyes.

Explanations will be given, but that does not negate the underlying fact; the world system will come towards a cataclysmic end. Most of these explanations being given come from *'the boardroom'* and somebody is just parroting them. *Hey Pastor you are really painting it grim. It cannot be that bad. It's not possible. What are the chances it's going to happen?!* In ordinary probability we could say the chances of this happening is 1. But since this is no ordinary probability we say it is 4 out of 1 that it is happening. But why should Old Nick pull such a stunt? Old Nick is not a fool as some suppose he is. He is a genius. An evil genius. But a genius still. The first thing he knows is that when the world system is approaching the catastrophic end, people will not take it lying down. They will do anything and go anywhere to get a solution. It is in times of adversity that new devils are born. **People become extremely wicked in trying times.** Satan works on the principle of Destroyer and Doctor.

Matthew 24:8 *All these are the beginning of sorrows.* [9] *Then*
shall they deliver you up to be afflicted, and shall
kill you: and ye shall be hated of all nations for
my name's sake. [10] *And then shall many be*
offended, and shall betray one another,
and shall hate one another. [11] *And*
many false prophets shall rise,
and shall deceive
many.

Look at this scripture carefully. The devil who is a **murderer** begins to kill God's people in verse 9. When the pressure is intense the devil who is the **corruptor** of minds brings division to the Christians verse 10, but that is not the end. The devil who started the killing spree is at the other end of the line, ready to receive victims of the new holocaust, as the **messiah** verse 11. But this is a false messiah. Have a look at the scriptures again. Though he is destroyer he transforms himself into a fake Doctor. And the unsuspecting, the gullible are caught in his Death Web. No one will look for Satan if all is well. So he starts a process the end very much known to himself and when things begin to swelter he provides a solution to an already morally depleted world.

Many children of God do not know the second thing that Satan knows. *The world was never designed to be ruled by presidents, prime ministers, secretary generals... no, no, no!* **The world was designed to be ruled by a king.** God's idea for the world is a spiritual monarch. A divine monarch. That is why all the political squabbles will not yield any lasting solution. God's order is for a king to rule the earth. This is no ordinary king for this king must be unique. *This king must be worshipped, literally worshipped.* He is the only one to whom the right to rule belongs after Adam fell. Genesis 49:10. Whether we jump and squawk we can't run away from this impending fact: we are headed, thanks to democracy towards **One World Government** and the devil's boy at the helm of power. With open arms he awaits us. And Satan his father, very much aware of that, with his system in place is impatiently waiting. **Believe it or not, love it or hate it nobody is going to escape the spiritual dimension of life. Nobody.** *(Did you read Matthew 24:9 properly? Why are Christians going to be hated by ALL nations? Because of the name of Jesus. Mark the word 'name', it's going to play a crucial role in these last days).* God's legitimate world ruler, Jesus Christ was unceremoniously thrown off the stage. Satan has his king too. We'll look at him later. But since the people are deeply desperate what happens? *What is the next solution since politics are failing us?* Satan has seen the desperation; he presses the red button...

B. Futile Pharisaism 2

Matthew 5:20 *For I say unto you, That except your righteousness shall exceed the righteousness of the scribes and Pharisees, ye shall in no case enter into the kingdom of heaven.*

For comfort, where else could one turn if not religion? The evil genius has done his homework. And he has done it to perfection. The devil has tormented people to the point of despair. As he sees the desperation, he points them to the Church as the solution. *Satan pointing people to Church?* Yes. *Then Satan is also born again! Halleluiah!!* Wait a minute Jimmy. Satan evangelizing for the Church?

Unprecedented occurrence. And people are coming. In droves. But as they come something should be observed. There is nothing the devil brings without a reason. These 'new comers' command God; heal me, God make me rich. Give me a great job. And throw in a sexy partner. And the N.G. (New God) asks, '*How d'you want your partner, male or female, two legged or four?*' Human or beast no big deal. '*Any,*' the fella responds '*just be quick I ain't got all day.*' The N.G. scampers across the planet to find a partner for his 'beloved Christian'. The fella throws in a tip in the offering bag and continues to drum his fingers on the arm of the pew, awaiting his order. With that the Tolerance Church is born. Thanks to the Pharisees they are seeing to it that things are so. And a hell less Christianity enlists more demanding membership. The informed and elite clergy knows if he or she does not give in to the demands they will not only lose a big following, they will be labeled uncouth and promoting hate speech. The haters. And no respectable clergy would like to be labeled a hater, right Danni? Good.

Therefore, pastors, like the sweet people they are give in and the scripture is fulfilled 2 Tim. 4:3. Discoveries are made to soothe the pain of the afflicted. Prosperity and sinless Christianity comes in. There is no need for pain in Christianity. And it does not matter what you throw away to avoid pain. Prosperity and success are the norm. And in the back of the pews the dear and much beloved Brother Devil thunders 'Amen'! Pulpits of hell, congregations of the dead multiply.

Proverbs 21:16 *The man that wandereth out of the*
way of understanding shall remain in
the congregation of
the dead.

The reason God created us is to worship Him. But notice something here, if you look closely, all the world problems today point in one direction, **worship**. All these problems we see are to bring you to one point—**worship**. You can jump, scream, yodel till kingdom come everything converges on **worship**. *Keyworth, we know you are crazy, but this leaves us without any doubt. There is no cure for you.* Thank you for confirming what I have always known. If you understand the world system, you know what I am writing about. Man is created to worship God, but if he cannot do it willingly before God, then he will have to do it by force before the devil. World problems are meant to force people to bow before Satan, that is why he is called great architect. Worship God or worship Satan, it is one or the other. Each one has a throne we are to bow before. It will either be willingly or unwillingly. Consciously or unconsciously, we are all bowing before one of these two thrones, right now. May you bow before the right throne, so that it does not cost you your life. Church is there for us to worship.

It is not for God to dance to our incessant demands. No wonder we are replacing true preaching with useless copies. We do not need motivational speakers. We need true worshippers both in the pulpit and in the pews. Especially in the pulpits. A motivational speaker can never lead a person in the presence of God Almighty. But a worshipper can. A motivational speaker cannot go beyond the human sphere because his words are confined to the earth. A worshipper carries with him the eternal Word of Life, words that pierce hearts, words that move mountains, words that scatter evil spirits...words of The Creator of the Universe and **words that scare Satan's henchmen!** Acts 4:17. A worshipper is led by the Spirit of God. A motivational speaker by his human frailties.

John 6:63 *It is the spirit that quickeneth; the flesh profiteth nothing: the words that I speak unto you, they are spirit, and they are life.*

What we are engaged in does not require us playing games. It's a matter of life and death. The Bible is clear. **The flesh or human nature does not profit!** No gimmick will work. So let's throw them away. *What will work for us?* The Bible says the 'words', meaning the **rhema**, is what will work. **Rhema** is the word in motion, the word spoken. The **words** of God are spirit and are **life. The words of the Lord are the LIFE OF GOD!** The life of God is in rhema, this is why we do not need gimmicks in the pulpits. Satan knows them already and in fact he manufactures better ones. Is motivational speaking evil? No. Is quoting Aristotle or Chaos wrong? I have no problem with that. We do not just need it in the pulpit. We need the Word of God. It is a poor substitute for the Word of Life. When you are born again you become spirit John 3:6. You are not born of a woman but of God. *I know this may take time to sink in.* Your life is supernatural. Understand what happens when you are born again:

- You are born of the Spirit
- You are born of God
- **You are born of the Word**

When you are born of the Word, you live by the Word. But if you substitute the Word for the gimmicks of man, the devil will be more than glad to keep you in Intensive Care Unit, a total victim. The devil loves false wisdom. If he can pin you down with it, the better. Understand you are now different. You have a nature that depends on God's Word, nothing else. This nature changes everything else. This is why the Bible says you are a new creation, with the mind of the Lord Jesus. 2 Corinthians 5:17,1 Corinthians 2:16. When we depend on human frailties we miss out and the devil is more than glad to keep it that way. You are spirit, born of the incorruptible eternal Word of God. Friend the supernatural is your life. Don't live on an empty tank! I am not against motivational speaking. I am not against God healing. I am not against prosperity. *Are we saying God does not heal today? Are we denying the healing abilities of God? Is God able to prosper financially today? Or was it only a sign or an example He gave a long time ago? Pastor this is confusing.* Patrick I have heard this debate before. In Africa we say, 'Don't finish your mouth.' Keep quiet. Yes, God does heal. If God could never heal today, He would not be God. Period. If God would leave financial prosperity to Satan while all his children wallow in abject poverty, He would not be an inch better than Satan! He would become a liar. A move, which I believe would displease Satan. For God would topple Satan as the Grand Master of Lies. Healing belongs to God. Finances belong to God. *Huh? Money belongs to God? Pastor my grandma is turning in her grave. That is not how I have known it.* Perry, she is gonna turn many revolutions before I'm through. Just tell her to rise. Money does not belong to the devil and we are going to look at it biblically. What Christians need is a healthy gospel. The gospel as it is, not the poor concoctions we are manufacturing. At our peril.

Look at the note of money in your hand. The paper you hold is a promissory note. It is a symbol of the real thing. Suppose you have a $10, it means in the bank there is either silver or gold equivalent to the figure shown on the note and in this case 10. The bank is not supposed to hesitate to give you silver or gold upon presentation of that $10 dollar note or bill. You cannot move around town with the all the silver and gold, why not carry something lighter? This is the idea behind money. The idea was stupendous, but… (*Let me solemnly admit that it is not that way anymore. There is no silver, there is no gold—the paper is worthless). Where has it gone?* Please don't tempt me to answer. Following the normal situation, the paper is supposed to be backed by silver or gold. But do you know who owns it all?

Haggai 2:8 *'The silver is mine and the gold is mine,' declares the* LORD *Almighty.*

Gold and silver which represent all wealth belong to God. Quit moving in rags and thinking you have become holy by being poor. That's warped thinking. Money is not evil. It is not. But the love of money is! You cannot love silver and gold and escape condemnation from God. Israel was not condemned by God for having wealth, in fact the power to acquire wealth comes from God. Deut. 18:18. God slapped Israel the time He saw them making wealth an idol. He stepped in to teach them manners.

Elvis, I am not against prosperity! Do I believe in prosperity? No. I believe in God who prospers spiritually, financially, physically...3 John 2. I do not believe in God who prospers you financially without consideration for your spiritual welfare. God does not elevate anyhow just for games. He cannot prosper you so that you sink deeper and deeper in the quick sands of riches. Many people want to use God. How dare you.

People cannot get saved without money. It's common sense *we need money*. A preacher has to use money one way or the other to take the gospel to the people. Money yes is vital, but it must be given its proper position—it's a tool. But because of the desperation Satan has attached to it many are losing their lives over money. The more you are starved from something the higher the craving for it. Satan is a psychologist.

However, many a Church leader has thrown the Bible out for cash. And what has remained? The devil. False teachings are coming up to make more money. If you want money, the Church is the fundraising point. You notice that today with every message preached comes the demand for more money. People are being charged to get healing. But the apostle Paul emphasized the gospel must be free. Free. Is the Church becoming a market? Maybe. We just don't know whether it's the marketeers who are in the Church or musketeers. Tell me the difference. It's pure showbiz.

A fat grin has just flashed across James' handsome face. He is nodding in agreement. As someone in ministry, I am very much aware of some fellows like James, whose hands cannot be pried from the coins in their palms. They would rather die a hundred million times than give something for God's work. Money is in their blood system. They never believe in the dead rising when you preach, but touch their money. Even if they are dead, they will rise for their money. They are born again, but the pockets are not. In fact the only born again thing about them is their sweet rolling tongue. Children of The Most High do not despair. He who began a good work in you will provide. The gospel will move on in the midst of greedy people. Money has power, yes. But that is the deceptive part. Money is a paper, which is wood, which is a tree. And in a similar manner that we tie dogs, horses and donkeys to trees, many in the Church have been bound or tied to this tree by Satan. What a pity. Take a note and look at it. Imagine you are missing God, you are headed for disaster because of that paper. Surrender to God now when there is still time. A dog or a horse which has been tied to a tree cannot go beyond the length of the rope or tether.

Realize that unless you change, you will never go far in Christianity because you are tied to money. You worship money. **And what you worship owns you.** Satan has said to you because I cannot stop you from going to Church, go, but do not go beyond the tether I have made for you

Exodus 8:28 *Pharaoh said, "I will let you go to offer sacrifices to the* LORD *your God ..., but you must not go very far.*

The devil wants you within reach. Money is causing casualties. The love for money is spreading from the pulpit to the pews.

Luke 16:13 *"No servant can serve two masters. Either he will hate the one and love the other, or he will be devoted to the one and despise the other. You cannot serve both God and Money."* 14 *The Pharisees, who loved money, heard all this and were sneering at Jesus.*

Church we need a balance on money. The Pharisees **insulted** Jesus because He corrected them on money. They loved money to the point of worshipping it! That's why He said you cannot serve two masters; one will be above the other. Is it only the Pharisees? Nay. We are breaking every Word of God today to get money. Meaning, the acquisition of money takes center stage. Friend you are becoming Judas. You are betraying Jesus for a few bills or notes. Turn around before it is too late. Remember the most foolish thing you could ever do is to say, 'Since I have already messed up, I might as well wallow in my mess'. We all have faltered, but we never stayed down. And we refuse self pity or condemnation because we have honestly repented before the Father of our Lord Jesus, who is also our Daddy. Do it now. Repent. A lot of doctrinal issues have arisen. What is so shocking today is the shallowness of the strong Christians.

I know I may be mistaken for some I know–it–all. I also know that as long as one has a brain they will have an opinion. *Even sick opinions.* It is very important to understand something in the Word of God. Not all problems come from the devil. No.

Matthew 7:25 *And the rain descended, and the floods came,*
and the winds blew, and beat upon that house;
and it fell not: for it was founded
upon a rock.

The Lord Jesus gives us a clear picture in the above scripture. There are two sources of problems. Some are 'rain' that finally form a flood, others are 'wind'. Rain represents the physical; some of these problems could even come about as a result of human error or failure or human greed or selfishness. But they all still cause great pain. The 'wind' represents problems that are spiritual; these are caused by the devil and his minions, the demons. But the truth of the matter is that the devil is always larking somewhere to take advantage of any glaring opportunity. And there is no better place where Satan has taken center stage like the church. **The first sign that Satan is in the Church is the desperation to accept anything at face value as being from God.** This is futile pharisaism at work. I remember an overzealous brother suggested we start Triple T.

'*What in the universe is Triple T?'* I enquired.
'*T*he *T*op *T*en', He said. I was all ears. I was clueless. He was speaking a language from Mars. He told me that it is done in the US of A. They pick the top preachers.
'Christians do this?'
'Yes.'

I let the issue rest. I didn't want to depend on hearsay. Then when I was watching TV it came up. Somebody was not happy because a close friend was not part of **'The Top Ten.'** I was now becoming interested. And a few days later when I visited a friend, my quest reached its climax. My friend had a paper, he was reading. When he put it on his sofa, I picked it up. I spotted something. My big African *ears* had *caught* something in the *wind*. In that paper, a US Christian paper, there was serious criticism of a particular Top Ten list because it catered for only a particular section of Christians.

Someone was writing to correct the mistake. The publishers (Christians) went on to list their own Top Twenty best preachers with photos! I never talked about it with my friend. But I learnt a lesson. *We have fallen from grace.* We are no longer looking unto Jesus the Author and Finisher of our faith, but unto the performance of the other. *Where are these intelligent ideas coming from?* We are now asking people to vote for us after delivering messages? Whose messages are we delivering, His or ours? The Apostle Paul would literally cringe at such rotten thoughts! How can you accept Triple T and thereafter teach that we are the body of Christ—we cannot all be the nose or the mouth we must differ but complement one another? Isn't that contradiction? I have never seen anywhere in the Bible where we are told to compete with one another and come up with such absurd ideas. **I don't care if something comes from Ghana, Japan, Malaysia, Iceland, Israel or the US of A. If it's unbiblical it is unbiblical!** *If I am better than you then the body of Christ is in a terrible state. If that's true Christianity I wouldn't want to be part of it. Not now not ever.* Are we not supposed to consider others better than ourselves? The Corinthian Church had a similar issue.

> **1**Corinthians 4:6b *...that ye might learn in us not to think of men above that which is written, that no one of you be puffed up for one against another.*

Pride divides the Church. May we loath the very idea of being mentioned in the top twenty. The world does that, but should children of God crave the crumbs from the tables of the world? The Holy Spirit knew this evil thing that's why He added

2Corinthians 10:12 *For we dare not make ourselves of the number, or compare ourselves with some that commend themselves: but they measuring themselves by themselves, and comparing themselves among themselves, are not wise.*

Competition among the saints makes them foolish. Our command is to encourage one another unto good works, not to compete. No wonder we are falling like flies in a house that has just been sprayed with insecticide. We have the wrong target. We have left the weightier matters and are focusing on trivialities. When you see a group of soldiers busy competing, just know they are not at war. Competition is not for soldiers at war, unity is! If this is not unbridled pharisaism, then there has never been pharisaism since creation.

A lot of Christians today think every spirit is from God. The origin of something does not make it scriptural. The Top Ten or Top Twenty is not godly. Just because something is from the US of A does not make it holy. It may be from the deep pit of hell. **Every messenger of God is Top One.** The devil is where he is today because of pride. We are doing the same. What is going on? Some ideas are being manufactured in Hell and we gobble them without checking. Today's Christian has never heard of familiar spirits. Or water spirits. And the devil is simpering with a Havana cigar in his left claw and a bottle of Mosi lager in the right. Psychology and familiar spirits have taken over the Church. Familiar spirits and psychology have replaced the Bible. People's futures have never been brighter with all the psychological mayhem in the pulpits. Only problem, the world is offering the original, the Church, a faded photocopy. No wonder. Many are constantly looking at their watches during services. They want to leave. They have appointments with better fortunetellers. The people know their pastor is fake, and the pastor knows the people are fake. And everyone is happy. The people, the pastor and the devil. Life is fair. The Church has reached the freezing point. This point is a Satan less Christianity. This Christianity is about love. God is love and anyone talking about sin is not moving in love. No more Satanism, no more witchcraft. After all, it is just a craft. There are many crafts... aircraft, hovercraft, handcraft no big deal. Today's true pastor is left with nothing, but sleepless nights because he is at pains to convince people hell is real. Some big shot with 2 million degrees in theology has just discovered through intense research that when the ice thaws in the poles, because of global warming, the fire in hell will be extinguished. And God will have a big problem looking for matches to start another hell. So hell is finished. God is love.

I have no such problem. I don't debate over real things. If someone refuses to accept the message, my advice is simple; don't carry a sweater as you go to hell, you won't need it, instead carry enough ice cubes to keep yourself cool. Religion, it must be pointed out, does two things always.

- **It unites in evil**
- **And it camouflages evil**

Religion is a license to do evil. More evils have been committed in the name of religion than in any other sphere of life. **Behind the smokes of confusion we see, lies the hellish fire of religion.** That's why Satan loves religion. *Note that I am not talking about Christianity but religion.* **Humanism is the heart of this religion.** Human beings and their desires become the centre of the new set up. Who needs God? **Humanism dear friend is the deification of man and dethroning of God Almighty.** Haven't you noticed that God is a light thing now? He does not carry that 'awe' effect anymore. God is a clown. This is what is in the Church. Prime Evil Religion. Sweet concoctions are made out of the scriptures to please the already inflated egos of people. Tell them they are going to prosper. Tell them if they could master their abilities, all things will change—mind over matter. It is all mental. Psychology remember? After all they are gods. The Bible calls them gods in John 10:34 We are gods hooray! But a closer look at John 10:34 reveals the opposite. Perhaps they are right. They are indeed gods according to

John 10:34 *Jesus answered them, Is it not*
written in your law, I said,
Ye are gods?

Jesus called those who were not of his flock—gods—those who were the devil's. A person claiming to be a god from John 10:34 must also courageously accept John 10:26.

John 10:26 *But ye believe not, because ye are not of my sheep, as I said unto you.*

Remember religion unites in evil. Humanism seeks the enthroning of man and the dethroning of God. What is humanism? **A concoction of eastern mysticism plus the careless hunger for mammon the god of wealth.** In Church people seek titles. People are not content with just being a pastor, bishop…in fact even BISHOP has taken on a new meaning of late. It's no longer a calling or ministerial function but a heroic status. Nebuchadnezzar was rebuked for imagining he was a god. The Babylonians could not be separated from the life of sorcery, horoscopes, hepatoscopy (examining livers) and other forms of witchcraft.

Ezekiel 21:21 *For the king of Babylon will stop at the fork in the road, at the junction of the two roads, to seek an omen: He will cast lots with arrows,he will consult his idols, he will examine the liver.*

King Neb became super big headed because he could run around *naked*, yodeling and chanting a few syllables. He mesmerized a few beings, but not The King of the Universe—Jehovah. God Almighty was so displeased with him that He sent him to the Rainforests of the Congo. And Nebuchadnezzar, the Great King of Babylon forgot the taste of cappuccino and vodka as he chomped grass in a way that provoked dismay and jealous from animals. The animals marched in protest to some NGO headquarters and the next thing we know; human beings were banned from eating grass. And just like that, Animal Rights were born.

Sir listen, you cannot be big headed for God. Impossible. He will bring you down. Before a few years ago you never existed. A few years later you will not. He remains. Wizen up. Herod was a great public speaker. Sensational orator. God slaughtered him in a manner which many cannot believe up to this time. They try to water down the fact that worms chewed him to death. Acts 12:22–23. Why? He accepted the title of a god. There is something about this demonic independence from God our Creator. It is more prominent than ever before and if not checked, it will sweep if possible even the elect. **I have said this before, the problem of sin is that it is sweet. It is only the results that are bitter.** Man does not wizen up quickly. The idea of gods has permeated from eastern religions. It's true we are superhuman. If you are born again you must be or else you are not born again. But there seems to be some kind of fissure. It's like the man who told me that we all worship the same God in all religions, after all we are all believers. *No wait a second. I know we are supposed to be nice, open minded, moderate, but which God? What do you believe in?* **The driving force behind the 'gods' business today is not the truth of who we are as born–agains, but a desire to become idols.** The conclusions of many preachers about 'gods' reveals the dark patches of being 'idols'. And many who are radical on the minor issues don't want to talk about some major issues. Are we majoring in minors? We want to prove we are not truly radical. A radical Christian is unreasonable and uncivilized. It is a weakness not to accept other views. **Great wisdom.**

Moderation. Moderation is what the world is calling for. A little Christian yoga. It is just meditation. Nothing wrong. Peace today is from yoga not Jesus. Spiritually blind people do not understand that yoga is more dangerous than a gun or a bomb. Am serious. **A gun can kill you but not decide your destiny. Yoga does both.** Yoga at kindergarten level looks harmless, but who doesn't know about the higher levels of yoga? John, have you been fooled? Don't you know anything about the higher levels of yoga? *Child, don't insult my intelligence.* I know the things I know. Listen, dear. You can play with a wild cub it's fine. But remember it's growing and so are its demands. One day it will have dinner. And you will definitely be the main course. Sin or wickedness trickles before it begins to pour. First you start nibbling at sin, finally all restraint cast aside you begin to gulp it. When they talk about yoga, they can only fool those who want to be fooled. Come on child open your eyes. In higher levels of yoga you connect with demonic forces head on. You leave the body into another world, the kingdom of darkness.

Before you get on any bus or plane, find out the destination. Only a fool jumps on board for fun. Fun in such moments always proves fatal. Pharisaism is what is going on. We are pleasing people and satisfying their evil appetites, at Jesus' expense. Aaron's excuse was that the people asked him to make them a calf. And he did. Most of us preach and teach about Aaron, but we live like him. The people before us are not different from those Israelites in the desert. They want calves and we have not disappointed them. The only difference, instead of making calves for them, we have made them into calves. Ready for slaughter. And they do not suspect it. *I wouldn't be surprised if I heard the devil has died because of excitement.* It's just too good to be true. He keeps asking his deputies to pinch him.

C. False Synergy 3

Proverbs 11:21 *Though hand join in hand, the wicked shall not be unpunished: but the seed of the righteous shall be delivered.*

Friend, politicians and the Church have failed to give the people the demands of their lives; therefore time for synergy has come. An ungodly synergy is in sight. Back to babel. *Where the hell is Nimrod to lead us?* It is very important to realize that even as we discuss there are three kingdoms caught up in this struggle. Three kingdoms, Docas. God's Kingdom, Man's kingdom and the Devil's kingdom. These three kingdoms have vested the future of the earth in the following leadership. There are four kinds of clergy and three kinds of presidency or governments. Let us start with the clergy.

(i) The Hireling John 10:12–13, Micah 3:11

This fella is in it for the money. This one will do all the ministerial functions as long as all is clear. Should there be a threat to his/her life or pain because of the Bible he/she bolts out of the place faster than a bolt of lightning.

(ii) The Idol Zechariah 11:17

He is the god of the Church. All the Church looks to him as the super star. He is omnipresent, omniscient, almighty god. The Church is personal property. He fires and hires and is never wrong. Any other opinion other than his meets a harsh rebuttal. He only appreciates those who have sleek tongues who can never correct or guide him to the throne of God, but to the throne of self, where he the invincible, immutable, unerring one abides. He has no heart for the people. He is the Church, even God the Holy Spirit cannot direct him. Self is all there is. The people have noticed it and they love it. For they are all like him and desire to be like him. He is highly reverenced.

(iii) Wolf Matthew 7:15, Acts 20:29

These are messengers of Satan. The first two could just be misguided, overzealous, and without understanding human beings. The wolf in real sense is one who, knowing he is the devil's very own, masquerades as God's messenger. The Bible says it is not strange if the devil's messengers appear like the true messengers of God. Now, here is where you slow down, you are about to hit a brick wall of truth. **You cannot always tell a wolf from the actions. A wolf is known by the motive. And motive can only be discerned. Spiritual gifts are needed now more than ever before.** That is why the Bible says test the **spirits** of the prophets. Discerning of spirits is a key factor in these last days. Actions alone will not help you, because you will never know who some people really are until you get their hearts! *But the Bible says you shall know them by their fruits, what are you saying Pastor Keyworth?* What I am saying is this. There are two levels of knowing. The first is by the physical, observation, the second is by the spiritual, discerning. Look at the scripture below so that you get it.

> Luke 16:15 *But He said to them, You are the ones who declare yourselves just and upright before men, but God knows your hearts. For what is exalted and highly thought of among men is detestable and abhorrent (an abomination) in the sight of God. (Amp)*

Did you see that Mike? Before people, they **declare themselves just and upright,** but God is seeing their deceit clearly. To be 'Just' is to be without blemish. You cannot put a finger on anything in their **public and** *private* **lives.** But away from your eyes and ears, places that no eye or ear reaches, they are devils. And because none can fault them they are highly revered. Are you getting this? **Clean outside, but inside they are tombs**. Welcome to post graduate Christianity. Now this is something we will touch on later.

(iv) True Shepherd Jeremiah 3:15

He is not in it for the money or the name. To him the work of the Lord is not negotiable. The work and his life are one. He is faithful. 'Faithfulness', my dear Tim is a very tough word. Faithful always means endurance or perseverance. You cannot say you have been faithful when there have been no opportunities to test your resolve. Faithfulness is seen in the stormy waters of life. Faithfulness is being steady under pressure. Riches, poverty, death threats even man's praise do not deter him from the goal before him. He loves the sheep and he is with them all the time. Sometimes the sheep are naughty, they are willful and even despise him, but he still loves them and he will not be dissuaded from his passion. The call.

All in all, that is the leadership we have from the Church. The first two are from the kingdom of man, the third from the kingdom of hell and the fourth from the kingdom of God. On the political and 'civil' leadership side there is representation from each kingdom. Three kinds of governance involved in a life and death struggle to rule the earth!

(i) Kingdom Of Man Hosea 8:4, Isaiah 7:5-6.

They have set up kings, but not by me: they have made
princes, and I knew it not: of their silver and
their gold have they made them
idols, that they may be
cut off.

This is just a group of men who feel they could wrest power from whoever has it to ascend to the throne. Their agenda is to increase their wealth. They have no people at heart. Every day when they wake up self and personal interest take center stage. You dare not advise them, you become an instant enemy of the state. Villain class one (VC1). The Lord

Himself expresses ignorance over this group's ascendance to the throne. He clearly states that He is *unaware.* **Meaning He does not recognize or sanction the person on the throne.** Understand this: the throne is holy, but the person on it is crooked.

(ii)Kingdom Of The Devil Psalm 2

There is an international conspiracy revealed in this chapter. Some wicked prominent people meet behind closed doors to plot against God and Christianity. Presidents are involved, but not all of them. These children of darkness are on the throne to fulfill the mandate given to them by their dad, Satan. It is not going to be all rosy for those who expect Christianity not to cost them anything.

(iii)Kingdom Of God Hebrews 13:1–8.

The person on the throne is God appointed. He or she carries God's mandate to rule. The throne in all the three setups belongs to God. And by throne we mean the authority to rule is from God. Let me point out something here. Some people may not necessarily be Christians but God okays them to rule at certain moments for His own good. Isaiah 44:28, 45:1. That is why Christians who only pray for leaders during elections are a big joke. You need to pray for your leadership all the time. That throne is in a life and death struggle. The devil would like to get it and rule. Having looked at the leadership we see that the enemy has set up a concoction of leadership. He is assembling a team to try to bring world rule to **one throne** in a systematic way. Satan has created a smoke screen so that we think we can get a solution for this world just as humans. But his commandos are in our midst. And they are not mere humans but spirits from the nether world.

Ezekiel 8:10 *So I went in and saw; and behold every form of creeping things, and abominable beasts, and all the idols of the house of Israel, pourtrayed upon the wall round about.*
11 *And there stood before them seventy men of the ancients of the house of Israel, and in the midst of them stood Jaazaniah the son of Shaphan, with every man his censer in his hand; and a thick cloud of incense went up.*

[12] *Then said he unto me, Son of man, hast thou seen what the ancients of the house of Israel do in the dark, every man in the chambers of his imagery? for they say, The LORD seeth us not; the LORD hath forsaken the earth.*

This is a secret society and it took the Spirit of God to reveal it to Ezekiel. People are seeking solutions from the devil. There is apostasy. A great falling away because people think God has forgotten them. *But is devil worship the solution if God has forgotten you?* The **elders** are in the occult. They worship demons but are trying to lead the people of God during the day, is it possible? *Let me help you get to heaven as I go to hell.* Not possible. They will pull you to their side. A come together party is in sight. The solution we are looking for has nothing to do with politics or religion we are told. We are going to help ourselves just as humans. That is nothing short of stupendous. I give the devil a clap. He is not called **The Great Architect Of The Universe** for nothing. He has this nice way of fooling those who want to be fooled. As an architect, the devil's system is now ripe and the people who cannot see it coming are the very Christians! If your target cannot notice your trap, you have a wonderful time before you. Things are going according to plan. For example because people are desperate, the enemy unleashes questionable NGOs. I am not against NGOs, get me right Anne. I am looking at some of them. Those that have a connection to secret societies. The questionable ones. These questionable NGOs dismantle any form of Christianity and say all religions lead to God. In fact, they go a step further and attack Jesus in many scandalous ways. But the masses who are constantly bombarded with numerous misfortunes and are already starving have no choice but to submit or face death. Then slowly all religions are being systematically forced into being one since *they all lead to God.* **One Religion One Hope.**

Listen the devil is putting in place a system to take over the media too. He is not leaving any stone unturned this time. **The one who controls the media controls the world by propaganda.** The prince of the power of the air is really ruling over the air waves. Tell the people what they want to hear and the plan will not fail. But that is where I seem to have concern. **Dear Paul, some things you read in newspapers, magazines, books, some things you see or hear on TVs**

and radios are designed for you to read, see and hear them, so that you draw up a wrong conclusion. Did you know that?

So one should not be naïve to think every religious book on the market is meant to help them, no. They are meant to keep you shallow or mislead you. Listen, it is not that the author does not know the truth, but that he or she knows the truth and wants to keep it under lock and key! **Someone somewhere is being paid to keep you ignorant.** *Sounds like a good career. Why in the world didn't I think of that first?*

> Ephesians 4:14 *Then we will no longer be infants, tossed back and forth by the waves, and blown here and there by every wind of teaching and by the cunning and craftiness of men in their deceitful scheming.*

Shallow books leave you where they found you, shallow. There is some noise made but there is no improvement. The question at issue is crystal clear: Are you mature enough to notice? The devil is evil but he is a genius. He is progressively implementing his system and the security guards are snoring. Poverty, diseases, wars, hurricanes, tsunamis have come upon the suffering masses like an avalanche. Their bewildered faces can tell, they are beyond their wits end. Let's look at diseases for example.

Everywhere you turn you see that man's hope is hitting the lowest meniscus level. Inexplicable diseases are sprouting, at a time when people have not finished dealing with other dreadful monsters like hunger and political instability. But why the sudden proliferation of these diseases? They are being manufactured in the pit of hell at lightning speed. AIDS, cancer, Ebola, Bird flu the world is tottering under their weight. Look at AIDS. AIDS is a multibillion dollar industry today. I can give you two reasons Terry, why it is going to take more than hell to find the **real** cure. Some of these diseases are multibillion dollar industries and finding the cure today is sending most NGOs to the graves.

Sam, not every NGO has you at heart. No baby. They will not accept a cure easily. They will not take it lying down. *It is better the cure is not found.* That is their conclusion. It must quickly be pointed out that in the midst of this melee, there are genuine NGOs; some have risked everything to reach out to the suffering. That is why you can only know who is who when you 'test the spirits.' Christian morals are fading as we grapple for a solution. Have you noticed?

Yes the world is easily beginning to squeeze Christian values out of us. We are conforming to the world, contrary to the Lord's Word in Romans 12:1–2. We are embracing the devil's world view. I remember having a discussion with a great man of God. He told me that we must let people use condoms; we must be loving and caring. I agreed.

'So when do Christians use the condoms?' I asked.

'There are certain times a Christian finds himself or herself in a tight spot, what happens? Get into your pocket or hand bag and fish out a condom. Don't you see that this will help a Christian live longer?' He educated me.

'Sounds good to me,' I responded, 'but I have a question. I am asking for your considered opinion.'

'Go ahead,' he said with a smile on his blessed face.

'Don't you think by carrying a condom, the mental resistance has already been defeated? Won't that produce a chain reaction of unstable behavior?'

'That's true, but I didn't mean that. I meant if one finds himself or herself in a room with another person of the opposite gender, then just walk down the street and get a condom and help yourselves, understood?'

'Crystal clear.' I said

'Good,' he responded.

After a minute or two I put my perfectly brewed cup of tea down, licked my lips, looked at my host and smiled.

'You have a question?' He asked
'Just a suggestion.'
'Go on,' he urged me.

'Don't you think if someone leaves the room to go and look for a condom on the streets, God has provided a way of escape for that person? Why should you come back when God has opened a door of escape? Isn't that what the Bible says about temptation in 1 Corinthians 10:13?'

He fixed his eyes on me for a few seconds trying to read the expression on my handsome face. He smiled and said, 'Clever young man. I was joking'. **He wasn't**. I am not against condoms, they are good, they make good balloons. And I am not ignorant of the **real story** behind condoms.

Never forget there are three citizens from three kingdoms. I refuse to be forced to forget what I know! The Church must not be judgmental and at the same time it must help people who are running away from dangerous vices like pornography, sexual exploitation etc. A person running away from such is not assisted when you hand him condoms. You are killing him. It is also true that because of an imbalance, our gospel has no love. We are abnormally critical of those who are doing their best. We focus so much on their weak moments. *We all must appear strong.* No. Jesus is the one who makes you strong. **Don't fake your strength. Jesus never died for the strong.** I have never seen it in the Bible. Today's Church has a false gospel; those who stumble are *disfellowshipped* because some big shot thinks so. But the big shot who has no sexual problem is busy hiding a drug addiction problem. If he had a sexual problem, he wants the baby Christian to overcome it in two minutes. Some teachers are, unwise. They spent twenty years learning something and they want the pupil to know it all in two minutes. Teach, teach, help the young ones then they will grow. **I know that some of the I–know–it–all perfectionists have a lot to hide.** If Christianity is by grace let's see how we could be of help to those who really need our help. On the other hand, there is the demonic tolerance. There is no restraint. It is 'All systems go!' No holds–barred sinning.

Ephesians 4:27 says let's not give license to the devil. Don't take grace for granted. If you are not careful, you are about to miss grace. Let there be a balance. I am not saying go and mess up Jesus does not care. He does. And He is judge.

Reason number two why a cure **may** not come soon for AIDS is easy to guess. If there is a cure, what will the Antichrist mesmerize the world with when he steps on the podium? Eliminating diseases like AIDS will make every Jim and Jack and Jane fall at the feet of the devil's son. **Even if by some sweet happening AIDS was eliminated, the devil will not take time to put another strange disease on the shelves.** While we are playing games with the gospel, the devil has cancelled all vacations and is even doing night shifts! We shouldn't be ignorant.

2 Corinthians 2:11. *"...we are not ignorant of his devices."*

God is watching what is happening. He can never be out witted, not by man and not by the devil. His Word stands. Choose whom you shall serve.

You are about to experience a phenomenon. All this mess that you see: the political mayhem and the circus in Church are a curtain raiser for the main event, The Grand Entrance...

II. Coming Of The Two Beasts

2Thessalonians 2:8 *Then that lawless one will be revealed whom the*
Lord will slay with the breath of His mouth and bring
to an end by the appearance of His coming;
9 *that is, the one whose coming is in accord with*
the activity of Satan, with all power and
signs and false wonders
(NASB)

A. False Picture 4

*Luke 6:39 And he spake a parable unto them,
Can the blind lead the blind? shall
they not both fall into
the ditch?*

HOLLYWOOD ANTICHRIST

For a long time now many people have been under the delusional impression that God is the one, who by some irresistible power of 'predestination' picked the Antichrist. That is erroneous thinking. We live in a time when the devil is drawing sympathy. What the masses do not know is that the master of warped minds has come up with a way of misleading many, and he is succeeding among the spiritually blind. God knows who the Antichrist is, but it does not make God responsible for his actions. **Foreknowledge is not causative.** The idea that is moving around where everyone thinks the Antichrist is a victim of 'fate' is pure rotten nonsense. On the other hand, yes I agree he is a victim of fate. **Fate** is a demon, do you know that dear?

*Isaiah 65:11 "But because the rest of you have forsaken the LORD
and have forgotten his Temple, and because you have prepared
feasts to honor the god of Fate and have offered mixed
wine to the god of Destiny, 12 now I will
'destine' you for the sword.
(NLT)*

He is a victim of what he worships. True. But it is not the Father of the Lord Jesus who picked or predestined him. The Antichrist is not a pawn or an innocent lamb. You and I have decisions and choices to make.

And that depends not on God but on us. That my friend applies to the false Christ. Do not even have sympathy for him. There is no sympathy for the devil's son.

Antichrist films from Hollywood have played a terrible role in 'theologizing' the masses with their own versions of the Antichrist. They depict a person born without a choice and a will of his own. The false Christ, in these Hollywood movies, is born already branded with 666, which everyone assumes is the mark of the beast. This person has no choice. From inception this person is evil. Nothing could be further from the truth. This view could be looked at, by a child of God from two angles.

Lack of the knowledge of scriptures is what is being displayed. When Jesus died on the cross he died even for those who were opposing Him and all who will oppose Him and the devil's puppy is included in the number of those given the opportunity of eternal life. 1 John 2:2. Sounds strange I know.

- Lack of knowledge of the scriptures—if one does not know the scriptures, it automatically results into error or deception. Hollywood's antichrist films have no biblical basis to depict the Antichrist as one already 'evil' from the word 'go'. Everyone in this world has a choice, including Satan's puppy—the Antichrist!
- The opposite possibility could be true—it may not be a lack of knowledge or an error. It could be a ploy to mislead the unsuspecting. The Church leadership is to blame for not teaching the people the truth. It hails some of these films that mislead.

So God is portrayed as being both good and evil since he ordains some to be evil and others to be good. But a study of the character of God repels this preposterous approach. The God of the Bible is not 'yin' and 'yang' god. No. The truth is clear. And I would like you dear to pay extra attention. **You are not human without a 'will' and a 'choice'!** The Antichrist is no such a being. Is he a programmed robot? The Bible puts all the false lies that the antichrist has no **will** to rest.

Daniel 11:36a *"The king will do as he pleases. He will exalt and magnify himself above every god*

and will say unheard-of things
against the God of gods.
(NIV)

The false Christ has a 'will' of his own. He does as he **pleases.** And pride is his middle name. He will be proud like his father, the devil. Now the nugget of truth we must embrace is the issue of who the antichrist is supposed to be. Who is this individual? Are you ready?

Luke 17:1 *Then said he unto the disciples, It is*
impossible but that offences will come:
but woe unto him, through
whom they come!

Evil has to come that is a fact, that is the devil's programme. Jesus says 'offences' will come. Offences are things that cause discomfort or unpleasant situations. Offences are also traps. Traps are coming. *The Lord Jesus has already cursed the person who willingly makes himself available to be used by the devil to trap others.* But is there a particular person determined by God the Father of the Lord Jesus to be the conveyor belt? No. The devil himself is a busy person to prove that there are no predetermined people for him. He is roaming around looking for someone to destroy. In the book of Job, he confesses and agrees with this scripture that he's all the time prowling for a victim. The devil's puppy, the Antichrist is the devil's worst victim since creation of man.

Proper perspective is very important. The position of 'Antichrist' Sandra, is an open cheque. Any person who proves himself 'worthy' to be given the throne of Satan will be offered. Note that the word 'worthy' could either be positive or negative. Would you like to take a guess as to whom Satan was eyeing to become his son? You are right if you said 'Jesus'. Luke 4. The devil offered the kingdoms of the world to Jesus. Because Jesus had proved himself a formidable foe, the devil had to placate him with a tantalizing offer. The devil spoke the diamond sentence: *I give it to whomever I wish!* The devil is a liar, but it does not mean he does not prevaricate. Here he meant every word. 'Whomever' means anyone. The devil's offer is one—**worship me**. To get the devil's throne be a worshipper. Satan worshipper.

It's common knowledge Jesus refused. But one thing still stands—**The Offer!** Many Satanists have tried in the past, but have failed lamentably to satisfy Satan. I am not labeling Hitler the monster a Satanist, though a careful study of his beliefs could really provide some exciting revelations, but the man had this insatiable hunger to be god. He declared himself lord of the Church and the state! No wonder he felt he could rule the entire world through murder and oppression. He felt he was the one to be the messiah for the world. I can assure you, it hasn't ended with Hitler. There are worse Hitlers on the loose. But there is one person who is going to rule the world, for even God will let it be so. He won't intervene as He has done before.

Clara there is one among the Satanists whom Satan has been eyeing. His voracious appetite for evil has whetted the devil's appetite for a son. Satan has been without a begotten son. Among the elite Satanists, is one whom Satan will reveal the greatest of all secrets in his hands.

Revelation 2:24 *...which have not known the depths of Satan...*

In Satanism there are some deep things. Deep evil. Many are engaged in these things. **(Many ordinary people are just seeing the tip of a giant iceberg. When we speak we are like mad people. We speak an 'insane' language. But we know beyond what they will ever know).** Satan will be so pleased with him that for the first time Satan will seem to like a human being. Satan will give him his own throne! Revelation 13:1–2. There are many levels in Satanism. The deeper you go the more power you have and the more wicked your heart becomes. Do not think all Satanists know everything. Most of them die in the lower ranks. It takes mad determination to get to the higher levels. The higher you go the more secrets are unveiled to you but the fewer the number. *The final human level belongs to two people.* Dread is their breath. These two men are going to be entrusted with the deepest secrets of Satanic worship. Many, right now are craving to be in that spot.

The last two positions in the occult hierarchy are called **BEASTS.** Yes. The two Highest Positions in the occult are literally called—The Beasts. The False Prophet and The False Christ. One is from the world religions and the other political. No one knows those two people apart from themselves. It is a closely guarded secret. These two have a personal encounter with Satan that no other person has ever had. **The secrets they hold could make your hair jump from your body. They carry an anointing, an evil anointing.** Without the Holy Spirit it is impossible to resist them. You can bet your last recession money. You cannot stand in their presence.

Unless we get into the Book of Acts our story will be incomplete. In the Book of Acts lies a great secret which many have not known and because of this, peril has come upon them like an avalanche. **Friend I am on my knees pleading with you. Don't you ever forget what you are about to read. Let it be etched on your spirit. I mean this with everything in me.**

SIMON—ACTS 8:9–11

Acts 8:9 **But there was a certain man, called Simon, which beforetime in the same city used sorcery, and bewitched the people of Samaria, giving out that himself was some great one:**

10 **To whom they all gave heed, from the least to the greatest, saying, This man is the great power of God.**

11 **And to him they had regard, because that of long time he had bewitched them with sorceries.**

He mesmerized the people of Samaria. In fact the Bible says he **bewitched them.** And instead of being exposed as a very evil man he was being praised! That is the power of deception. It leads you to embrace a starving lion. Some versions say he bewitched the city of Samaria. Others use the expression, 'the country of Samaria'. **The point is this; the degree one reaches or attains in the occult determines the level of geographical influence.** Suppose Simon stood for a position in public office, every Samaritan would have killed to have him as their leader. It is not very different with the Antichrist. What is just different are the operational levels. **Simon had a national level**, the Antichrist is above that. **Satan's son is going to have a global influence**. He is going to be revered like no man has ever been. Let me put it this way. The anointing upon him is going to be so real, tangible, that looking at him makes one feel insignificant. He will carry with him an aura of great power, indescribable power. You cannot just say 'oh antichrist I won't bow to you'. No. No. His presence is breath taking. You feel like falling before him—**to worship him.** His demonic anointing is so great, he will prove a great genius too. His level of intelligence will be a great factor in crowning this man 'god.'

Remember the system is supposed to go wrong and this is the man who puts the puzzle together. **In Jesus dwells the fullness of the Godhead. Colossians 2:19. In this man dwells all the fullness of Satan.**

> Revelation. 12:3 *Then another sign appeared in heaven: an enormous RED DRAGON with seven heads and ten horns and seven crowns on his heads.*

And

> Revelation. 13: 1 *And I saw a beast coming out of the sea. He had ten horns and seven heads, with ten crowns on his horns, and on each head a blasphemous name.*

The first scripture is describing the father, while the second is talking about the son. In this boy is the sum total of evil. He has no problem with simple diseases like AIDS that are manufactured in his backyard. He is the Messiah. The king of the world. What Jesus refused to get, this man will—world power through devil worship. No wonder God will just pick him alive and throw him in the lake of fire. All Satanists will look to him as their big brother. They'll lick their wounds and wonder what he did right to get the job they have all been eyeing.

Every person is faced with a very important question to answer. In one of the most powerful Business Administration scriptures in the Bible, the Lord Jesus spoke this…

> Mark 8:36 *For what does it profit a man to gain the whole world, and forfeit his life [in the eternal kingdom of God]?* 37 *For what can a man*

give as an exchange (a compensation,
a ransom, in return) for his [blessed]
life [in the eternal kingdom
of God]? (Amp)

We all have to face this question head on. No one can ever claim to have ignored it. We all answer it by the choices or decisions we make. Some choose to forfeit their lives to get a few crumbs from Satan, while others are diehards who refuse even to sniff at what Satan has to offer. The *scents* from hell give them the urge to vomit. The Antichrist falls in the former. The Lord Jesus cautioned people to carefully consider The Cost and Profit of any business transaction. Is getting the whole world under your sway worth eternal damnation? This is a clear warning to all those who desire to ascend to greater heights using wicked means. **And the Antichrist has been warned.**

B. False Christ 5

Revelation 13:1 And I stood upon the sand of the sea, and saw a beast rise up out of the sea, having seven heads and ten horns, and upon his horns ten crowns, and upon his heads the name of blasphemy. [2] And the beast which I saw was like unto a leopard, and his feet were as the feet of a bear, and his mouth as the mouth of a lion: and the dragon gave him his power, and his seat, and great authority.

From the scripture we see that the beast hails from the sea, from the underworld. The 'sea' here symbolizes the people. It could also imply instability and **sin**. Isaiah 57:20 and Jude 13. What better way of entering for the devil's child than for the moment when everyone is crying for solutions? The child of darkness will come at a time when there is great need for leadership. And ten Kings or presidents or political leaders will hand over their power to the beast. They will become his subordinates! **The G10 will sell you out to the devil's puppy! Revelation 17:12–13.** *Bright future in the kingdom of darkness huh? Fantastic.* He will look harmless, but friend he is the devil incarnate. And this is where I would like you to understand a very serious point. Let us take the **spiritual center of 'sin,'** the nether world to understand the flip side of the sea. I would like to inform you that some of the worst spirits that have plagued mankind are from the 'seas'. The worst familiar spirits are water spirits. The most intensely trained Satanists are from the 'waters'. The title of antichrist does not just mean one who opposes Christ. That is the kindergarten part. **The core of Antichrist is to be an impostor!** He is coming to prove he is the real messiah. That is why the beast is not only a **venomous** beast, but a TRAP. He comes as a trap for many. The experience of King Saul gives us a clear picture how these insidious familiar spirits operate. We see God and Saul are not on talking terms. Let me unveil a few points why I believe the fella that came was not Samuel but a demon.

A familiar spirit. And the reason we bring this up is because the Antichrist has the anointing of a familiar spirit. May God Almighty the Father of our Lord Jesus deliver you from this trap. This poisonous animal. He may appear gentle and show a bit of love by his solutions and makeshift generosity but rest assured he is pure poison. **Sometimes we define** *generosity* **in spiritual matters as 'spiritual bait.'** Live wisely.

King Saul

1. **<u>When Saul asked God for an answer God refused.</u>** When God has refused he has refused. When He gives a 'no' find out why He has said so by carrying out an introspection. In 1Samuel 14:38 Saul did exactly this, but here he refused to do it. Why? Saul knew exactly why God could not give him an answer. God had already given Saul an answer but Saul didn't want God's answer. He wanted another one! **David was that answer.** The Philistines feared one man, David. And David was at Saul's disposal. He was a humble servant. But jealous gnawed at Saul's heart like cancer. What Saul never knew was that by divine wisdom God's solution is what was keeping him in office. By chasing David around the planet, Saul was chasing himself out of office. How wise God is. Just like today, if you despise Jesus and ask for another solution you ain't gonna get it, but a demon yes, a familiar spirit you will get.

2. **<u>Saul did not want to acknowledge the sin in his life, so he looked for another solution.</u>** This is our trend today, we refuse to let go of our sins, but insist on getting answers from God. *Which God?* By going to the witch, Saul was not ready to leave David alone. And he was not ready to repent for the murder of God's priests. No wonder God could not answer him.

3. **Many times, we have spoken on behalf of Saul.** It is better to get it, as they say, from 'The horse's mouth'.(Today's horses speak). Let's ask him.

Saul?

Yes?

Since God can't speak to you what do you want?

A familiar spirit.

Did you hear that? He said it. **Familiar spirit**. Look at it in verse 7. What is a familiar spirit? It is a spirit operating like the Spirit of God, but not really the Spirit of God. Remember the scripture, Satan pretending to be an angel of light? Saul just said , 'I want the devil to appear as an angel of light and give me a solution'. *Pastor Keyworth you are kidding.* If it were possible I'd have loved to. Saul's request is the request of an insane man. Look at what he said. *'Look for a woman to deceive me'.* **A woman with a familiar spirit was a woman who could call or summon a spirit of the dead at will.** With all his eyes open he went for it. *Sister, God is sovereign, He will answer you by tarot cards, horoscopes or Ouija boards.* How sweet.

4. **Saul disguised himself and moved in the dark** because what he was doing was

- Evil in the sight of God.
- Evil in the sight of the Israelites
- Laughable in the sight of the enemy

This is the world syndrome. If God does not answer me I will anoint my answer as having come from God. Saul was saying since God can't answer I'm going to raise Samuel from the dead and ask him for the answer. Kindergarten stuff. **By whose power is he coming up?** By the devil's power. Saul is a genius. **He passes God by, goes to the devil to ask for power so that God could answer him to defeat the devil.** Read that again.

5. **Saul became 'God' when he revoked God's decree against wickedness.** Now you can see why God didn't want to answer him.

He could cancel God's command as if he were greater than Him. Verse 10.

6. **Now Saul has gone very far.** He takes the name of God in vain by swearing in wickedness. Friend that is guts! Super guts!!

7. **The woman acknowledges having power to bring up the SPIRIT of anyone mentioned by Saul.** This is demonic power not God's power. Verse 11.

8. **This is very interesting. The perspective we get is not of a child of God**. The witch is the one who claims Samuel has come. She puts up an Oscar winning performance and we all herald, she has seen Samuel**. She does not claim interruption by a higher power, instead she exclaims, 'you are Saul!'.** I don't need to go to Cambridge or Harvard University to know it is Saul. Only a fool wouldn't have known it was Saul. It is preschool common sense that

- No one had the **audacity** to promise security or her safety unless he was either very close to Saul or he was Saul. She was not stupid to risk her neck for nothing.
- **She was a liar**. A terrible liar. She knew Saul's voice. Saul was not speaking to her by telephone. His voice was not muffled. Tom, you know your president's voice, don't you? Without seeing him you can tell. Acts 12:14a. You can know someone by his voice.
- **Necromancers are not dumb**. They know their clients even before their clients approach them. They can even tell you who you want to talk to. Am I lying? We are not ignorant of the devil's devices. She played the crazy Saul very well. She played him! Apart from her stunt to shriek she continued with her life as usual. This whole charade has nothing to do with God. **He never intervened. If God had intervened He would have destroyed her paraphernalia.**

9. Friend we are seeing why God never answered Saul or intervened in any way in this matter. **The great king Saul who refused to depend on God's word is seen now guzzling the devil's word, hook, line and sinker with stunning appetite.** He accepts the devil's word. Listen, it is either you are getting God's Word or the devil's word. Whether you

like it or not you live by the Word. That's how we are designed. We are to live in touch with the supernatural. But which supernatural?

10. **Saul had a particular 'form' he wanted**. Listen. The devil is a good chef. He will give you with all garnishes your dream order. On that, you can count on his expertise. Saul is once again told by a witch who has not seen anything unusual in her séance (which would have led us to believe God had intervened) that Samuel has come. Saul wisely, like the genius he was, **Perceived, Convinced, Deluded** himself it was Samuel! Listen. This is spiritual warfare. **Before the devil deceives a person, there is usually some deception that person is already entertaining.** Saul had a **form** of Samuel he already wanted. And that's the form that came! This has nothing to do with God. Familiar spirit. Don't forget.

11. **Saul, the man who had refused to bow his heart before God is now seen bowing before a demon.** Saul forgot this important truth; **Humility is your position in God, not your posture before the devil.** Any humility outside God is not humility. If God cannot give me an answer man cannot, especially a dead one! Saul was in occult worship. If today we tell people God is sovereign, he can answer through Ouija boards then we have sacrificed the entire generation to the devil. Because many are waiting for the slightest signal to retrieve them from their wardrobes!

12. **This Samuel and even Saul agree on one thing, it is Saul by the séance (which is a prayer to the devil) who brings this Samuel up. Saul again acknowledges God cannot answer him.** Reality check. **Who has answered him then?** Saul goes behind God's back to consult 'Samuel'. Interesting. The other day I heard a renowned man of God say, 'There are many ways to God. Jesus is **just** one of them'. I can see John's eyes are bulging he wants me to comment. I will behave like a politician and say, 'No comment'.

13. The demon Samuel spoke to Saul, but his heart was too darkened to get the sense. The demon point blankly told him, **'If God has departed how can Samuel answer you?'** It never clicked in Saul's head. This is what he had requested. Find me a woman to deceive me. And he was not ready to change.

14. **This is where you see the cunning nature of the devil.** He spoke half-truth and that truth did not point to his business. This is where you see this is not Samuel. The devil's answer hid the part that would expose the evil of necromancy! 1 Kings 20;42, 1 Chronicles. 10;13. If the demon had exposed this, the devil would have lost business in the sight of the witch and Saul's evil associates. The business of consulting the dead was untouched. The devil couldn't shoot himself in the foot.

15. What the demon Samuel spoke is not new and not extraordinary in the kingdom of darkness. This is a crucial point in the kingdom of darkness. **This is The Point Of Invitation or Offer. This is the territory of the demon Chemosh.** An Invitation is a suggestion or offer from a person to **save** his neck by the help of the devil. In devil worship everyone and anyone is dispensable except you. Your father, mother , daughter, son, wife or husband are all potential sacrifices! The devil knows many when confronted by impending death, choose to save their necks and offer another person's neck. 2 Kings 3:24–27. It is the devil's prerogative to accept or refuse. He is extremely vicious on former Christians.

16. **Why did God really kill Saul?** God killed him, when He withdrew His Spirit and the devil who comes to steal, kill and destroy moved in for a kill. The real reason God killed Saul was because he **never** inquired of the Lord.

'Come on, Saul did inquire.'
'Friend Saul never did.'
'Then what did he do?'

Let this be a lesson to you.

a) Do not come before God with pride. Saul refused to acknowledge the sin in his life and came before God as if all was well. It takes a fool to courageously march on in sin. The problem with sin is that it is not always bitter. It has a sweet taste. The consequences are the ones that are bitter. Saul maintained his murderous attitude towards David. Saul and Cain must have been identical twins! They are very identical in their intentions. They both wanted to kill the righteous. Their principle was the same. *If I'm wicked we must all be wicked.* They refuse to change and kill those who change.

b) Do not come before God if you already have plan B. When God did not answer Saul he simply turned and found himself a witch. We have so many Sauls today. As they pray, they are already contemplating plan B. James 1:5–8. Psalm 7:9

c) Saul did not really enquire from God because he wanted only the solution while he maintained his evil ways. But God was more concerned about a relationship with him than anything else. Saul did not understand the principle of stewardship. God only protects that which is dedicated to Him. What would God be doing protecting the devil's property? And from whom?

17. The **fact that Saul had murdered the priests and probably thrown away the urim and thumin does not still make God unable to reach Saul.** There was another option God could have used. Dreams. **God could not have substituted dreams for a witch.** God hates any form of witchcraft. What you have just seen my friend is the law of reverse strategy. The devil brings Saul to the level of constant sin. **When the devil wants to trap someone with familiarity, he ceases to attack him.** Saul became so familiar with God that God ceased being the King of the Universe. Everything was okay. Then the devil launched the attack. The philistines gathered. This time even day old babies and grannies wanted a piece of Saul.

Listen my friend. **The power of sin is guilt. Guilt brings fear before your adversary.** Only the righteous before God are bold. **It is hard to be courageous before Satan with sin on your shoulder.** And because you know, you have been sinning willfully you find it hard to seek God's help and you go to the same devil for a solution. The Philistines were serious sorcerers, king Saul was aware. What he wanted to do was to counter their power using this medium's power. **You cannot attack the devil's child using his father's resources**. By coming under Satan's covering you have automatically lost your position. The one you want to attack becomes your superior. You have been recruited ingeniously.

Saul is scared as the chapter concludes and we see him getting into the dark night. That reminds me of Judas, after eating. He left and it was night. Light is only found in the path of obedience. **Before the devil**

attacks a person, he first lets them hate, despise, chase or flee from that which God has ordained as their help. King Saul did just that.

Examining the life of Saul is one way of getting a glimpse of how familiar spirits operate. The Beast from the Sea and the Beast from the earth all work under this spirit. Many believe Saul brought up Samuel, because God is sovereign. Yes, God is sovereign. But what are the **Key Words? Familiar Spirit.** It looks like the original. It behaves like the original, but it is a **FAKE**. That is when spiritual gifts come in. The Word, says **TEST** some spirits, others let them pass unchecked? 1 John 4:1. What we are told to pass through the test tube is what is claiming to be of God. Anything godly take it to the lab. *Now you know you are a scientist in the Lord. Congratulate yourself.* But as you test you must have the standard to compare with.

Church, the Antichrist is not coming to out rightly oppose Christ. That is the kindergarten part. Here is the mask he will wear. He will come as Him! He will say he is **The Messiah** and he can prove it. **And if the Antichrist is coming as Christ, then he is coming with Another Gospel.** There is another gospel on the horizon. It is a familiar gospel. **It looks like the real, but alas, scrutiny reveals it is like one of those counterfeits from China. Fake product.** You cannot lean on it. We must really be aware of counterfeits. If the familiar spirit that came to Saul could confuse us, we might as well go and make peace with the Antichrist, for we are finished. We are dead meat. We are no match for the devil's first son. The devil cannot believe his luck.

Hell has sent its ambassador. Just as Christians are ambassadors this man is an ambassador from hell. We need to understand what is going on. So let us begin to dissect this boy from hell. His father tried to destroy God's Son but failed. He tried to destroy Israel, but failed. He went and established a kingdom. Many people are puzzled that the antichrist and the devil's kingdom could be associated like this in this scripture. Yes. Whatever God does Satan copies. *The devil must have been very intelligent at school. Imagine a fella whose life is all about copying.* Dan, where is the kingdom of God today? Wonderful. In you. In a similar manner what you see is the very embodiment of Satan's kingdom in this wicked man. What he is coming to do is to **introduce devil worship** at another level. **It is all about devil worship! Pull down God and His Bible and enthrone**

Satan with his satanic bible. Friend, it is all about worship. Nothing else. These simple Satanists that are around will appear like his ball boys. Where is he coming from? Among the elite. For the Bible says the elite will gather and begin to oppose The Great I AM.

> Psalm 2:1 *Why do the nations conspire and the peoples plot in vain?* 2:2 *The kings of the earth take their stand and the rulers gather together against the* LORD *and against his Anointed One.*

Rebellion is in the air. Grand rebellion. There is an international Conspiracy against God and Jesus. This conspiracy is complex, for it touches all areas of society. It has nothing to do with race, gender or nationality. This is why I have no headache when boys and girls run around claiming they found Jesus having sex with Mary Magdalene. And a few witnesses come and give evidence that after all Jesus never even died, he fled to the East. It does not bother me, not even a bit. This international conspiracy will be very prominent among the **'world elite.'** God sees this as a joke. So do I. God is inviolate. You can neither attack Him nor harm Him. But we see that they want to get at God by harming you and liquidating Christianity. Christianity is under intensive attack. And what are we doing? Moderation. Why? They want to appease those who can't even be appeased. By moderation I have seen great men and women of God undoing the labour of other believers. Please them, at your peril. What we do and say will either qualify us or disqualify us. Please man or God. It is up to you.

It is common sense the Messiah has to come from Israel. I believe enough documents are in place to forge this demon—possessed man into power under that pretext. He may be Jewish or has enough evidence for back up. His vision will be to hijack Rome and Jerusalem. Europe will definitely be the next world super power, the revived Roman Empire at work. And Jerusalem is the religious capital of the world. The future for the unbelieving is chilling. Do not under estimate this evil man's power. Cultic leaders have power. Abnormal power. What this man will do, no human being has ever done. He will directly stand and speak against any god, starting with the Christian God. Listen, the devil lives on photocopying. He is a photocopier. Christians have been given gifts which they unfortunately debate and throw away. At their peril. God says in His sweet Word

> Luke 21:14 *Settle it therefore in your hearts, not to meditate before what ye shall answer:*[15] *For I will give you a mouth and wisdom, which all your adversaries shall not be able to gainsay nor resist.*

Settle it in your hearts. I will give you a mouth!!! Has He given you a mouth? **You have a supernatural mouth.** A supernatural mouth has three **main** characteristics

- **It declares and things happen**
- **It speaks in tongues**
- **It is not limited to the physical sphere**

Even in our society there are people who speak things and they happen using the devil's power. The devil has given them a mouth too! Your mouth is your gateway to success. But the devil is not that dumb. He has given the Antichrist something also, a counterfeit.

> Revelation 13:5 *And there was given unto him a mouth speaking great things and blasphemies…*

This is not a simple man. He can read your mind in a trice. The anointing upon him forces you to bow. On your own. In Christianity we have what is called **Grace**. What is grace? Grace is **Divine Ability** and Grace is also **Favour.** This wicked man has demonic ability to do whatever he pleases. But what is dangerous is his **ability to attract people's 'love'**. **Favour!** He will be so *loved* that anyone who utters just a syllable against him, many are willing to crucify without trial. Remember Simon in Acts 8? He was revered. But this fella is going to make Simon's record baby stuff. From the pit of hell, Simon will look at this man with envy. Simon will peep, from the pit of hell with unbridled admiration. This guy is not a toy soldier. Christians will come against him, but he will smile and slaughter them. He will kill God's people the Christians with great joy. Then he will extend his hand to others and say, *'I don't want to* *fight. Let's be a team'.* **Friend there is no wonderful moment like that. What are you made of? What will you say? That is the moment of truth.** Opposing him is clear death. No question mark. World finances are under him. Food shortages are not new. The devil has the ability to affect the world elements Job 1:16, 19. **Apart from that he has enough sons and daughters in certain places to fool the world with fake shortages.** When he creates problems his son is going to be a Joseph, he will provide the solutions. When there is a famine, he will provide the solution, but only his people must eat. Debates have been raging like wild fires whether it's true some products and food stuffs have been branded with 666. Many scrutinize barcodes and come up with some clues.

Some things being put across are pure psychiatric cases, but not everything. Others for sure have been branded. But is this not the mark of the beast? It sure is in some sense. Christians are confused about the mark of the beast. Why should they be? One says the mark of the beast is this. Another says it can't be, it is this. **The mark of the beast, the physical mark is still being perfected by various overzealous children of the devil.** After all the various forms we have seen, then the final is what will become the devil's official seal. **And that final seal is what the Bible has given us, not the process!** So many Christians and other observers are correct, but they all want to pull down the findings of others. We are behaving like *blind bats.* The devil is proud to begin putting his label on food. He wants the world to know who is in charge. I am glad to say, he is not! I know the devil and he knows me. We have an understanding. He is under my feet. And we are both comfortable leaving it like that. Will hunger separate you from the love of Christ? **Many have not understood what the Spirit was saying through the Apostle Paul in Romans 8: 35.** The *hunger* here, is not about missing breakfast because you are going for Bible study. No. This is where you are being forced to bow before the devil because your family will starve to death if you don't. If you look at the scripture, the first to be affected are the breadwinners. We will look at this later. Is somebody getting this message? **Your faith may be strong, but look at your child, your wife, your husband, and your feeble parents; will you let them starve to death because of some stupid, religious unbeneficial belief in some mythological person called Jesus?** Will you not do something for them? I hear the words of the Great Master,

Luke 14:26 *"If anyone comes to me and does not hate his father and mother, his wife and children, his brothers and sisters—yes, even his own life—he cannot be my disciple.*

Halleluiah!!! What is He saying? **Jesus is saying, if the worst came to the worst, and you have only one option, this is what you must bet your LAST on, ME.** Friend what we call Christianity is about to undergo a litmus test. But

John 16:33b "*…take heart! I have overcome the world."*

The solutions for world peace are vested in him. You don't have to know John 3:16 to see it coming. The world problems are going to intensify to the point of total collapse. When he comes on the scene he will pretend to be an angel of light for some time. But you and me know it is impossible for Satan to maintain being an angel of light—it's not his nature or character. Whenever he pretends, he's trying to win confidence from the gullible. The devil may give you all you want as long as he has you in his claws. When his son introduces a new level of Satanism it will either be The Word and face The Sword or Recant and Freedom. But what is *freedom*? Or should we put it this way; **Who is freedom?**

C. False Prophet 6

Revelation 13:11 *And I beheld another beast coming up out of the earth; and he had two horns like a lamb, and he spake as a dragon.* [12] *And he exerciseth all the power of the first beast before him, and causeth the earth and them which dwell therein to worship the first beast, whose deadly wound was healed.*

Forerunner and master strategist, this man comes from the earth unlike his master who comes from the sea. Though inferior in rank this is the most dangerous man between the two. This is the ingredient Satan had left out in his first attempt to annihilate Christianity and Israel. This fella is very dangerous. **Handle with care.** He is a cultic leader. A special cultic leader. Many cultic leaders have come and gone, but this one is the sum total. There have been great cultic leaders who have mesmerized multitudes before. Leaders who were regarded as heaven sent when in reality they hail from hell. This is one of them. And the greatest of them all.

A puzzle seems to confront us. **What is the difference between coming up out of the earth and out of the sea?** *The Bible is confusing.* Many throw in the towel and say the book of Revelation is unrevealing. It is very revealing. The Bible says he comes from the earth, while the first beast comes from the sea. The **sea** the Bible tells us is the general populace as revealed in Revelation 17:15, though we had taken a closer look at the literal 'sea' to get more insight. But our focus now is on this second beast that comes from the **earth**. What does this mean? We really don't have to sweat Gina; the Bible tells us something in

> Revelation 12:15 *And the serpent cast out of his mouth water as a flood after the woman, that he might cause her to be carried away of the flood.* [16] *And the earth helped the woman, and the earth opened her mouth, and swallowed up the flood which the dragon cast out of his mouth.*

Looking at these two scriptures we see that the **'earth'** is a reference to the **'friends'** of the **woman**. These are the ones who stand to aid her in the various struggles and challenges as it avoids being totally annihilated. But from these **'friends'** comes the **beast**! The second beast. **So from the** *earth* **that helped the woman in Revelation 12:15–16 comes this super betrayal!** Another question arises: who or what is the woman?

Scholars differ on this. There are three main schools of thought on this. The first group believes this is the Church, the second believes this is Mary and the last group believes this is Israel. I believe it is Israel and not the Church and definitely not Mary. Let's quickly look at this woman, Israel. In

> Revelation 12:1 *And there appeared a great wonder in heaven; a woman clothed with the sun, and the moon under her feet, and upon her head a crown of twelve stars:* [2] *And she being with child cried, travailing in birth, and pained to be delivered.*

Israel has had the privilege of receiving two Covenants or Testaments, the first is the one represented by the moon. It is past. Now she is clothed with a much higher one, the Full Light of Truth. God has revealed His blessings to mankind through Israel. This is the Sun the woman is clothed with. The twelve stars represent the patriarchs of Israel**. Note that the woman gave birth to a male child who is Jesus.** The Church never gave birth to Jesus, but Jesus is the one who gave birth to the Church.

Israel is blessed with being the nation from which the Messiah, the world ruler comes. As a nation she brought forth this man. Jesus. But from that moment, Israel has never ceased to have problems, why? The devil is mad for it bringing forth Jesus.

Psalm 83:3 *They have taken crafty counsel against thy people, and consulted against thy hidden ones.* [4] *They have said, Come, and let us cut them off from being a nation; that the name of Israel may be no more in remembrance.*

Before Jesus came Israel went through enormous pain. And in His infancy Israel was still under intense pressure. And after that Israel has been going through it. The Bible is clear on this and even declares **salvation is of the Jews.**

Romans 9:4 *Who are Israelites; to whom pertaineth the adoption, and the glory, and the covenants, and the giving of the law, and the service of God, and the promises;* [5]*Whose are the fathers, and of whom as concerning the flesh Christ came, who is over all, God blessed for ever. Amen.*

Evil having failed to totally annihilate Israel has devised another strategy, the extermination of the offspring. He begins to persecute all those who have been birthed from the promise. The promise that has been fulfilled by the coming of Jesus. The Christians. The Christians are the offspring of Israel, too.

Romans 4:16 *Therefore it is of faith, that it might be by grace; to the end the promise might be sure to all the seed; not to that only which is of the law, but to that also which is of the faith of Abraham; who is the father of us all*

The promise might be sure to all the seed and it goes on to state the seed, the seed according to faith. Already we see a set up here. Israel and Christians are on the receiving end. The Church never gave birth to Jesus, but Jesus gave birth to the Church. The twelve stars, the moon, the sun and the offspring all disqualify Mary from that spot of being the woman. And despite her going through pain Mary was not persecuted by the devil. At least there is no record of it in the Bible. But Israel has borne it. And God has carried Israel on eagles' wings before, but this time He says the woman will be given wings of a great eagle. Signifying the abundant grace with which He will deliver and still does deliver Israel. Israel knows what pain is. That lunatic Hitler did all he could to wipe it out of the face of the earth. And that is just one example. And from that moment the devil has been trying to hide his next step in destroying these people. The false prophet is just the man for the job.

Preschool betrayers like Judas will fall down at this university professor of the Faculty of Betrayers. This guy makes Judas a kindergarten boy in betrayal. But who qualifies to be 'The earth?' Who is always there for Israel when it needs help?

- **The West**
- **Jews in Diaspora**
- **The Church**

But to be specific this man is a combo. A combination of the three. As a prophet he is definitely religious. So he has the smell of a man of the cloth. And as we let down our guard especially in the Western Churches we have a pure recipe for disaster right before us. And he must be Jewish because the Jews or Israel will never acknowledge someone non Jewish as their prophet.

Religion is one channel the devil will use in capturing Jerusalem. The false prophet will capture many. By capturing Jerusalem, he captures three groups of people—The Jews, The Muslims and The Christians. He traps them into unification. For the Jews Jerusalem is the holiest city, the Moslems their third holiest city and the Christians? They were birthed from there and they look forward to the coming King who is to rule from there. And on top of that, they think of the heavenly Jerusalem. It has a great meaning to them.

(i)A Man Of Peace

There is no war in his tongue. That is why he has horns like a lamb. You can bet your last coin on him to be a Nobel Peace prize winner. He is going to be highly respected. I hope you still have Luke 16:15 in mind. He is very subtle. But remember he is a beast. Why? You will soon find out.

(ii)A Man With A Rolling Tongue

This fella has a sweet speech that after talking to you, you would think of buying him a Bentley, although you are fully aware he has just swindled you. He has a supernatural mouth. A demonic mouth. He speaks like a dragon. Speaking like a dragon means two things.

One of the greatest factors of subtleness is being able to show the victim what he is going to benefit, but fully aware that it leads to death. The serpent was subtle and went for Adam and Eve. He made the woman doubt God's word. Then BANG! **He is so sweet with his tongue that he makes you doubt what you already know**. He will present his offers in a tantalizing manner. He uses reason to capture the ignorant. How did his dad present his trick to Adam and Eve? Keep this in mind: **No man since the world came into existence has lied like the Antichrist and the False Prophet will.** These fellas are only second to the devil. *That's a whole lot of lying.* His speech is soothing. **You are mesmerized by his speech. This man and the Antichrist will fire all speech writers. They don't need their speeches written. They just flow. Fantastic public speakers! And the masses flow with the tide. The tide to hell.** But beware, under all that sweet talking the devil is up to something. I don't need a prophet to tell me what the devil wants to do. I know already. He comes to steal, kill and destroy. When the devil comes what does he want you to do? The devil wants you to focus on two things.

- How you have been unfairly treated by a loving, all powerful, God.
- How sweet and beneficial the thing you have been kept from is.

This guy is the master of temptations. He has perfected that art.

> James 1:12 *Blessed is the man that endureth temptation: for when he is tried, he shall receive the crown of life, which the Lord hath promised to them that love him.*

This scripture could read, 'Blessed is the person who **perseveres** under the **pressure** of temptation'. **A temptation is usually** *the desire of your life,* **brought at** *the wrong time* **using** *wrong means.* Our Lord, Jesus was tempted with the kingdoms of the world.

People think Jesus did not desire the kingdoms. He did. **A temptation is not a temptation if it is not appealing.** If someone tells you to drink gasoline, would that be a temptation? Yes and no. If you are a person definitely no, but if you are a vehicle fine. Jesus desired the kingdoms. Let's not be religious. Jesus wasn't a robot. That is what he came for. It was His desire and His Dad, who is your Dad had promised Him. Revelation 2:26–28. But the means He totally rejected. Temptation is a means to get out of God's will by your response. Temptation is an advertisement. Temptation has two sides, but truth has three.

Temptation.

- Shows you the desire
- Shows you how you have been unfairly kept from getting it

Truth

- Truth says okay I admit I have this desire
- Yes it has taken time for it to come
- Could I know who this concerned citizen is, who has called me?

Hell immediately hangs up. Tom, what interest does the devil have in your interest? Jesus gave us the secret of the devil, he comes to steal, kill and destroy. This son of the devil will mesmerize itching ears.

> Genesis 35:4 *So they [both young men and women] gave to Jacob all the strange gods they had and their earrings which were [worn as charms*

against evil] in their ears; and Jacob buried and hid them under the oak near Shechem.
(Amp)

The unfortunate thing is that the charms in people's ears of nowadays are repelling God's Word and making them receptive to demonic speeches. The devil has found a receptive people and he is not about to disappoint them. This man is the total package of a wolf in sheep skin—deadliest deceiver. Vs. 11.

- He is Jewish. This is what makes him more deadly. It is not all Israel that is called Israel. We are just about to learn the shocking truth about this scripture. Israel will only accept a prophet from Israel. He impersonates and rolls in one most great men of God.

Look at this

- He places himself as forerunner; John the Baptist vs 12
- He presents himself as the Elijah who was to come vs.13
- Numbers people as if he were Moses or Aaron
- Speech like the dragon, his father: subtle Gen.3 and 2 Cor. 10:4–5.

He wins world approval as final prophet, and then unleashes his boorish powers. After winning the world by all the miraculous power he displays, then lays it all in an age when humility is as rare as a unicorn, he says, 'I am not the messiah. I must decrease he must increase. The messiah is that one'. What grand entrance for the devil's puppy. Understand that as a prophet he will foretell the future. Did you get that? He will predict the future. Some people think when someone predicts the future then that person is sent by God. Here is the rebuttal.

Evil is not going to be initiated by this man. He is not starting afresh. He is only coming to up the game. The advance party has already come. Clubs, which people are calling churches are already teaching part of the doctrine. And not only the doctrine, the miraculous things are happening too. The Lord has not kept quiet, He has given us a clear warning. Standing orders.

Deuteronomy 13:1 " *If a prophet or a dreamer of dreams arises among you and gives you a sign or a wonder,* [2] *and the sign or the wonder comes true, concerning which he spoke to you, saying, ' Let us go after other gods (whom you have not known) and let us serve them,'* [3] *you shall not listen to the words of that prophet or that dreamer of dreams; for the* LORD *your God is testing you to find out if you love the* LORD *your God with all your heart and with all your soul.*

The test of a true prophet is that what he says comes to pass. *I wish.* **Not always.** The Bible is saying if a prophet arises from where? **Among you.** It is always easier to work from within and not from outside. *Brethren, pray for your pastors, priests, all those leading you. Pray as if that was your last prayer on earth.* If a stranger with some funny appearance comes and is preaching some strange gospel, who would believe him? None. But if someone close, someone among us is secretly pulled aside by the enemy, enticed and taught another gospel, it is easier to mislead many! The most complex thing I have seen is that the doctrine being preached is the bait the devil is using. Nobody will say let us go and worship another god openly. It all starts with the doctrine or teaching. Some smart Christians think a person who is being used by the devil cannot mention the name of Jesus. Shockingly unfortunate. We do not question certain things not because of our spirituality, but because of

- Blind loyalty
- Love of evil
- Or we have been bewitched!

You cannot blame your shallowness on lack of knowledge of scripture. You must study. **If your life depends on something, that thing is super priority!** There is no excuse for being shallow. You cannot let the devil toss you to and fro. For how long? We need intensity in our Bible study, now more than ever before. When there is false doctrine running wild, what do you do?

Deuteromy 13:14 *then you shall investigate and search out and inquire thoroughly. If it is true and the matter established that this abomination has been done among you…*

We must know whether someone is teaching with little knowledge or he is the devil's advocate. If he is the devil's advocate, then we watch our steps. We are not talking about being blockheads. We may differ in some things, even ministering, but the heart of the message must not differ. We are gifted differently, we must accept that. **But when we see a significant divergence from the Word of God we must** *Investigate***,** *Search out* **and** *Inquire thoroughly***.** Believe it or not the mystery of lawlessness is not a one day trap. It has been going on and we are approaching the climax- the final dimension. No wonder the false prophet will find it comfortable. Easy, relaxed, feeling at home.

This man will speak like a dragon. Speaking like a dragon involves flattery. Junk load of flattery. **You see how you are going to benefit, but very unaware how soon you are plunging down. The second meaning of speaking like a dragon is being unquestionable.** When he starts revealing his beastly qualities he will set up a Church organization or system that is not flexible. Rigid. When he says 'a' everyone has to hum, 'a' if you don't, your neck is on the chopping board. Our Nobel laureate will start chopping heads and instead of seeing something wrong with that, people will cover him in saliva, kissing him for a good job perfectly executed. **He is the man vested with the plan for the classification of the world.** A religious man, who looks harmless but inside he is full of the devil. Friend this man will perform miracles, but he is totally wicked. **Have you ever asked yourself why judgement will start from the Church? 1 Peter 4:17.** Let that ring a bell. And when he comes, this final man in the line of the devil's prophets, will categorize the world…

D. Final Touches 7

Hebrews 11:10 *For he looked for a city which hath foundations, whose builder and maker is God.*

Finishing touches are being put in place for the coming beasts. The Bible says the beasts are coming with false miracles. Does God perform miracles today? That is His nature. There are no false miracles without the true miracles. It's common sense. But I would like you to understand the underlying factor. The Word of God is full of miracle power. It is like dynamite. Bring flames close to it and there will be an explosion. You will not need to negotiate whether the fire will be there or not. The heat will create an explosion.

If there is a disease, the Word and the flame of your faith will bring down the wall of disease and knock it out of your life! The Pharisees did not know this about God's Word. They underrated the power in the Word of God. Many believe Jesus is coming—which is a far greater miracle than receiving a cure from Him. The Word of God has power to change any situation. The Word of God will bring you wealth. You can have anything.

Now our only issue is not to segment the Word of God to mean only one thing when it says a lot. A balance is important because some people would look down on those who don't have as if they are evil. Some people have even erroneously taught that *certain heathens* who have used God's principles are blessed by God leaving the faithful people in the Church. **Don't insult those who are faithful before**

God to promote a person who is not faithful just because he has promised you money. *What are we doing in the pulpits? Tell the people the real truth. Some of the people you promote are actually in the kingdom of darkness. And their wealth? It came from the devil. If you have nothing to preach go home and sleep!*

As we try to impress our 'sponsors' who even hate Jesus we try to look down on people in the Church just because they seem not to offer us more than the unrepentant outsiders. **Are we not prostituting ourselves?** The amount of wealth you have is not a sign of your faithfulness, otherwise some of God's faithful people would rise in protest. Some people who have been more faithful than you still own nothing, just some strings to cover their naked bodies with.

Hebrews 11:37b *They went about in sheepskins and goatskins,*
destitute, persecuted and mistreated— 38 *the world*
was not worthy of them. They wandered in
deserts and mountains, and in caves
and holes in the ground.

Lack in the lives of these great people is not what caught my attention. What blew my mind away was the 38th verse. **It does not say they were not worthy of the world, but the world was not worthy of them! The world was very cheap for them!**

That is why they couldn't own anything. They lived in caves and mountains and holes in the ground. They were very expensive for the world. They owned nothing because what they saw on earth was too cheap. **If you have something don't you dare insult the one who doesn't have. (And if you don't have and you are content please do not see demons in anyone who has. Let's appreciate the diverse gifts and ministries we have received from God).** Elijah a mighty miracle worker had to be kept by a struggling widow. *That does not paint a proper picture especially in our prosperity message set up today. A true prophet struggling in life? No limousine? He must have sinned or he has unbelief.*

One thing is crystal clear. We are approaching Break Point. Wealth is ours! **The time has come to get all the wealth we can get as children**

of God. The time has also come to be ready to be able to walk away from all of it at anytime with nothing, but threads of cotton that cover our bodies and the flaming Word of God in our hearts and hands! But there is something very dangerous I have seen and it is very fascinating. It is on miracles.

Matt hew 12:24 *But when the Pharisees heard this, they said,*
"It is only by Beelzebub, the prince of demons, that this fellow
drives out demons." 31 *And so I tell you, every sin and*
blasphemy will be forgiven men, but the
blasphemy against the Spirit will
not be forgiven.

United in crime the Pharisees proved a great force against Jesus, but failed completely short of matching Him. They hated Him deeply. And because of that they started even insulting the Spirit by which He operated although they knew He was a holy man. Pilate did not have to go to Oxford or Harvard to know they envied Jesus. Matt. 27:18 The result? The Pharisees were committing the unpardonable sin because even when they knew the power by which Jesus operated, the power of the Holy Spirit, they ascribed it to the devil. That is dangerous living.

Call it the greatest twist, today people are doing the opposite. We are ascribing the work of demons to the Holy Spirit! **People, with full knowledge of the operation of demonic forces are ascribing such miracles to God, the Holy Spirit. This is unpardonable.** We must be very careful or else we shall perish. This is one truth you must never ever ignore. If there is ever a time when God's children have been susceptible to the spirit of prostitution or deception it is now. **How can a pastor strip for church members and everyone says it's okay, she has the anointing?** And that is not a onetime event. **What anointing are you seeing? How can people stage prophecies and when it is discovered holy men of God say 'keep quiet'?** But how do we keep quiet if you are manufacturing prophecies to promote **Satanism**? I use the word **Satanism** literally. *Keyworth is this happening right here on earth?* No darling, why should it happen here, it is happening on Jupiter. Unbridled whoredom.

Hosea 4:12 *A spirit of prostitution leads them*

astray; they are unfaithful
to their God.

Some of our leaders have put an unnecessary emphasis on certain topics and have neglected the rest of the counsel of God. Truly we have become money making machines. Without sounding offensive and not stepping on more toes, I humbly say we have replaced wisdom with craftiness in the Church! **The devil is now very uncomfortable with some Christians, because they seem to be heading for his seat.** Their wickedness has sent huge tremors down the devil's aging spine. Soon there is going to be a coup de tat in the devil's kingdom! The devil anticipating this has just doubled his security. *Can't blame him*. Friend your soul is the prize in this battle. It is either Jesus will have it or the devil. Your future is in someone's hands, Jesus or the devil.

How I pray that we open our eyes to the new gospel and notice what it is all about. We must see through it. We are telling people not to be born–again, we say we are all children of God. Let's come together more offering. Hooray!

Everyone is a child of God? Whether someone is born–again or not, all mankind is God's family? That is unbiblical and very demonic. Back to Babel. The devil is trying to mislead you. The condition to be God's child is stated in John 1:12. **Any other way is no way but a figment of your over working imagination.** And as you walk with Jesus desire to be like Him, the Holy Spirit will be there to help you. Any human being has

- A spirit
- A soul
- A body

Someone who is born again has a soul, a body and a new spirit! He has a new spirit and the Spirit of Jesus Christ. Fallen man is under the household of Satan. Yes. That is how bad it is. Friend there are only two individuals since the world was created who will change the course of this world. These two individuals are compared below. They can't both be right and they cannot both be wrong. One of them is right the other false. Choose one today.

COMPARISON OF CHRIST TO ANTICHRIST

CHRIST	ANTICHRIST
1. Lamb Jn 1:36	Beast Rev. 13:1
2. All Authority Matt. 28:18	Great Authority Rev. 13:3
3. God gives Him Throne Rev.3:21	Satan gives Him Throne 13:3
4. Power Matt. 28:18	Power 13:3
5. Died and rose Rev.1:18	Dies and rises 13:3
6. Jerusalem capital	Jerusalem and Rome capitals
7. Leads a Monarch	Leads a Monarch
8. Claims to be God	Claims to be God Dan. 11:37
9.Does not marry	Does not marry Dan.11:37
10. Forerunner with Elijah spirit Matt.11:12	Forerunner with Elijah spirit Rev. 13:13
11. Worship His Father-God Jn. 4:23	Worship His Father –Satan Rev. 13:4
12. Worship Him Matt. 2:2	Worship Him 13:4
13. Rejected Jn. 1:11	Accepted 13:3
14. No beginning Micah 5:2	Has beginning
15. Has seal Jn. 15:16 and Eph. 4:30	Has mark, Name Number 13:17
16. No material possession Jn 7:53-8:1	Owns great wealth Dan. 11:38
17. From Above Jn. 3:31	From beneath Rev. 17:8
18. King Matt. 21:5	King Dan. 11:36
19. Has no end Heb. 1:8	Has end Rev. 19:20
20. Rejected kingship from men Jn. 6:15	Receives it Rev. 17:13
21. Forerunner killed. Matt. 14:10	Forerunner kills. Rev. 13:15

III. Categorizing Of The World's System

Revelation 13:16 *And he causeth all, both small and great, rich*
and poor, free and bond, to receive a mark in their
right hand, or in their foreheads: 17 *And that no*
man might buy or sell, save he that had the
mark, or the name of the beast, or
the number of his name.

A. False Prophet's People 8

> Revelation 13:3 *And I saw one of his heads as it were wounded to death; and his deadly wound was healed: and all the world wondered after the beast.*

From the scripture above we see that the world **'wondered'** not **'wandered'** after the beast. The devil's son is going to take the world by storm using the supernatural from the occult world—imitating the resurrection of the Lord Jesus. By rising from the dead Jesus has been declared the Lord of All because even death cannot hold him. He is Lord of life.

And that is what the devil's puppy is coming to imitate. Power over death. This will blow the minds of people that even atheists will believe in 'god', the devil's puppy. All those who have not believed in the resurrection of Jesus will believe in the resurrection of the Antichrist. There is no neutral ground. One has to choose. And you can never postpone it.

Look at the secret of God revealed here. This is very touching. You cannot afford not to shed tears. When you look at the many souls engrossed in unrighteousness and being carried away.

> 2Thessalonians 2:11 *And for this cause God shall send them strong delusion, that they should believe a lie:*
> 12 *That they all might be damned who believed*

not the truth, but had pleasure
in unrighteousness.

If you did not accept the truth God will let the devil deceive you to your damnation. Do not play around with salvation. Never ever play around with salvation. Friend you are on the very edge. Beware. The set up for the coming wickedness has reached unbelievable levels. I am not trying to alarm you but inform you. And what is most shocking are the players the devil is using.

Sin is controlling many lives today. Sin is taken lightly. Sin is what will make people accept with eagerness the lies of the wicked one. **God's secret is this: you have not believed the truth, so believe the lie.** And the reason you are believing the lie is because you love darkness! **God has discerned the hearts of men. They love wickedness.** When people talk lightly about Jesus I am not moved. The only thing that moves me is that I have been to a place they have never been before. I know what I have seen. And it is not pleasant. I feel sorry for them. Very sorry for their futile thoughts. Psalms 94:11.

Events that are taking place in the world today, show clearly that we do not have to wait for long for the wicked one to appear. **In fact there are a lot of clandestine meetings being held for this person to be revealed**. God will not help the wicked to know Jesus. He wants to see how far they can go with their hero the man of sin. **What is also appalling is that these strong delusions that God has permitted the wicked to perform are not in future but have already began in our days.** A brother approached me and told me about this powerful man of God. Whatever he tells a person it must be done. God speaks to this man. So he told one lady to leave her husband. Because he was seeing a bad future for her. So the woman left. The brother before me seemed excited. I didn't mince my words. I told him that his so called super man of God was no man of God. I told him that it was most likely the fella had been eyeing the woman and he wanted to jump into bed with her. The brother was very offended. He left an angry man. It didn't take long, the pastor was in some *chompy chompy* activities in bed with the sister. *Seeing a bad future for her? A man of God whose word cannot be questioned?* That's not brain washing, at least the brain would be clean. **That's brain damage!**

People love to be deceived. They just feel good when they are deceived. The deception was not in the *chompy chompy* issue in bed with the sister, but in being unquestionable. **There is no man of God whose word cannot be questioned. No person's word cannot be questioned. No one.** Whatever a person says could be questioned. That is not wrong. We are not robots. The Bible says even if an angel comes and delivers a strange gospel we are not to believe, what about a man or woman on earth? We are all to be questioned. Questioning is not bad. It is how we learn. **Gulping everything we hear without checking is not a sign of being spiritual, but a clear sign of mental defectiveness!** *Pastor, this man of God came to me and told me to sleep with him. Now I am pregnant. These men of God are fake.* And you daughter of Jezebel are not fake? Did he tie you? Were you not a willing participant? Did he come as an incubus? We know your mother, Jezebel. The apple doesn't fall further from the? *Tree.* Thank you John. If a pastor or whoever comes to you and asks you to sleep with him or her, simply decline. And pray for such a one. But what do we see nowadays? Many relish such moments. Before the pastor even finishes his demonic request, they are already out of their pants! Evil is just in them. Maybe they could have even been sending wrong signals to lure the pastor. What I just gave you is the lighter side. There's another man of God who had a tendency of exposing the nakedness of people as he prayed for them. When they fall 'in the spirit' he stops you from covering them. He was interested in the nakedness of the women. In fact he would touch the breasts of women and squeeze a little as he prayed for them. He was highly reverenced. Listen. Listen carefully with your spirit. There is no place in the Bible where we are told to be drunk! Except one place. Let me give it to you. *Before I do that all those under 75 years, close your eyes. Or better, go and sleep. This is not for children. Ready?*

> Proverbs 5:19 *Let her be as the loving hind and pleasant roe;*
> *let her breasts satisfy thee at all times;*
> *and be thou ravished always*
> *with her love.*

'Ravished' means to be 'intoxicated'. Drunk to the eyebrows! *But Pastor Keyworth, that scripture is referring to her love not her breasts!* If you are standing sit down. Or lean against something. (*I have dealt with this* *in detail in another book).* The word **'satisfy'** means to **'soak.' Do you know what it means to** *soak***?** Are you sure you want me to continue? Let her breasts do what to you? May God forgive you for being ignorant. The next meaning for the same word 'satisfy' is to **'make drunk'!** *Such things are being taught in church?* I see the religious taking nails and poles to crucify me. It's not me who said it, it's the Holy Spirit! **Friend, the Holy Spirit knew what He meant when He put in that word!** Here is the connection, let's not lose track. The guy was misbehaving in broad day light! He was getting **drunk**. For me no matter how anointed the man they talked about could have been I believe he was a wicked man. Especially that he could even expose the nakedness of some women as he offered them 'deliverance'. Yes people stumble, but there is a difference between one who stumbles and one who is looking for opportunities to stumble. **In fact some people create opportunities to stumble. A sinner is not one who has stumbled, but one who creates and desires to stumble and actually stumbles all the time. Proverbs 4:16.**

One must come to the point of true resolve. If one does not take a serious step to intensify one's relationship with the Holy Spirit that person is doomed. The Holy Spirit **'respects'** your nakedness. I repeat, the Holy Spirit respects your nakedness! These are biblical basics. When Adam and Eve came to know what nakedness was, God covered them. God does not like indecent exposure of one's body. **And God will not undress you to get healing or let the pastor molest you to be healed**. Come on. We know the Holy Spirit. He lives in us He talks to us. Every time something is trying to move you don't move unless it is God's Word. If something does not conform to the Word don't swallow it. We also know that nakedness is a big deal in Satanic activities. Some demons they summon cannot come until there is nakedness.

Please don't insult our intelligence. We know what we know. Period. A miracle is not always a sign of God the Holy Spirit's presence. Some people think every miracle is from God.

Revelation 13:14 *And deceiveth them that dwell on the earth by the means of those miracles which he had power to do…*

How can we be so simple? **God says because you do not want the truth you will find the lie your haven.** *Pastor what is the topic?* The False Prophet's People. Who are they and what is so special about them? It is very imperative for us to understand why things are happening the way they are. **Some people who have sworn allegiance to Satan are pushing the devil's agenda. These people have purposed to convert the world by whatever means. When one joins one never leaves.** You swear to be killed in a very cruel manner and stripped of everything should you even try to leave. In fact they have a spiritual gauge to see if you are slowing down in your participation. Friend welcome to reality. **We talk about the mark of the Beast all the time. But do we really know what we are talking about?** A lot has been said about the mark. Some say it is a micro chip. And we know in some countries like Spain dogs and cats are required by law to have chips. And there is a good spread across Europe and other parts of the world. A serious consideration has been made to do it on humans! It is true there are micro chips that once injected may be operational or functional from 99 to 120 years and they can never be removed once inserted. If you are 40 it will be with you until you are 139 to 160 years old. If you carefully consider the reasons being given for the chips to be approved, they are fantastic ideas, but *are they the real reasons?* Hmm. **The question of the millennium is this; Is the chip the mark of the beast?** It is possible but very inconclusive. The mark, the second dimension cannot be hidden. It must be visible for all to see! **But one thing I do not doubt, the micro chip system is part of the devil's system to control the world. Experiments have been made in higher places of wickedness to implant in humans these chips which are the size of a grain of rice. All those implanted have no privacy. Everything they do, say or whisper, every detail is gathered at a certain command center.** In English, they are under the ALL—SEEING EYE, BIG BROTHER! *But Pastor Keyworth the technology for such is not there.* Oh thank you for that correction. Let's wait for the official announcement. The devil is going to announce in seventy years from now that he has now finished the preparations and could all the good boys and girls line up to receive the sweet and nice mark from papa. **Dream on.**

Revelation 13:17 *And that no man might buy or sell, save he that had the mark, or the name*

of the beast, or the number
of his name.

The Bible talks about

- **The Mark of the Beast**
- **The Name of the Beast**
- **And the Number of His Name.**

Three very important things. Every individual will be required to have the mark. But there are others who will go beyond the mark. *Huh?*

Every person will be required to have the mark. But the mark is the first level. The Bible mentions three things, the mark, name and number of the Beast. 666 is not really the mark. **The mark, the name and the number are like the colors of the rainbow, distinct yet seeming to merge or fuse. I endeavor to show the distinction in this book by God's grace.** For you to get a clear picture keep in mind that Satan does not originate he copies. What he sees God doing he copies. Satan counterfeits what God does. Satan is the father of piracy. Let us start this journey from the Old Testament.

Ezekiel 9:4 *And the Lord said to him, Go through the midst*
of the city, through the midst of Jerusalem, and
set a mark upon the foreheads of the men who sigh
and groan over all the abominations that
are committed in the midst
of it. (Amp)

God commands the angel to put a mark on some people. Now this is where you must get it or else what follows will be pure jargon. What was God's criteria for giving the mark? Did He say, 'All short people 5 foot 2 and below should be given the mark and anyone above no mark?' Or did He say pick a particular skin tone, those on the darker side are the ones to receive it? **The mark was given to those men (and women) who were not happy with the system of their times.** They groaned over the sins. The people mentioned here had the fear of God and kept themselves unspotted by the world they lived in. **Sighing and groaning** could also mean they had even prayed for God to deliver the wicked from the snares of the evil one. They had interceded. What is so important to notice is that the driving force to see good and their hatred for wickedness were the factors God considered before giving them the mark.

The Mark was put on those who already had the desire. **The mark was the confirmation of what was already in them.** There is no forcing here. The mark was simply the confirmation of what was already inside.

Mark: What Does It Really Mean?

'Mark' means many things but there are two definitions that pervade the scriptures. It is these that I lay great emphasis on. The first is the Hebrew word 'Tau' and it means

- **A Seal**
- **Signature**
- **A sign of servitude**

It shows whom you belong to. Or whom you serve i.e. whose slave you are. The second is the Greek word **'Charagma.'** It means the same thing like 'tau.' But what is interesting about charagma is that it is very close in meaning and actually shares the same root word with the word **'charakter.'** And when you talk about **character** you are talking about an **'exact copy'** or **'express image.'**

Hebrews 1:3*Who being the brightness of his glory, and the express image of his person, and upholding all things by the word of his power, when he had by himself purged our sins, sat down on the right hand of the Majesty on high*

Jesus is the express image of God. The words 'express image' mean 'exact character'. **Mark is the character or nature of the one you willfully and genuinely follow.** And the bad news is, there is no neutral ground. **It is important to realize that this issue of the mark has never been done away with in Christianity.** Christians have a mark. **If you do not have the mark, Jesus said then you are not His.** But what is the Christian's mark?

Mark For Christians

Ephesians 1:13 *In Him you also who have heard the Word of Truth, the glad tidings (Gospel) of your salvation, and have believed in and adhered to and relied on Him, were stamped with the seal of the long-promised Holy Spirit.*

Did you see that, have you already been **stamped**? You have God's stamp or seal. A seal was the King's very signature. God's signature is on you. God's mark is upon you.

Ephesians 4:30 *And do not grieve the Holy Spirit of God [do not offend or vex or sadden Him], by Whom you were sealed (MARKED, branded as God's own, secured) for the day of redemption (of final deliverance through Christ from evil and the consequences of sin). (Amp)*

This one puts it in black and white that 'the seal' is the mark! *(Do you know that the first to receive the mark in our family is Jesus? John 6:27).* But it also reveals the mark. **The Christian mark is the Holy Spirit. The Holy Spirit is a PERSON**. He lives with us and in us. *The mark of Jesus is an invisible person.* Dear this is very important. Understand this very well. The mark is invisible. What does the Holy Spirit do in the Christian's life?

Purpose

The main purpose for the Holy Spirit is to change you into Christ's likeness. He wants you to have the very image of Jesus Christ in you. The Holy Spirit enables you to resist the influence of the world upon you. The Holy Spirit connects you to God the Father. He gives you free access to Dad. Look at this friend, you may have taken this for granted.

Characteristics

> Galatians 5:22 *But the fruit of the [Holy] Spirit [the work which His presence within accomplishes] is love, joy (gladness), peace, patience (an even temper, forbearance), kindness, goodness (benevolence), faithfulness,*
> 23 *Gentleness (meekness, humility), self-control (self-restraint, continence). Against such things there is no law [that can bring a charge].*

What we call the fruit of the spirit is actually the very nature of Jesus. That is who Jesus is! You can read that scripture like this: But Jesus is Love, Joy, etc. but why is the Holy Spirit doing all this?

Reasons

To present you spotless to Christ. Jesus is coming for a people that are like Him, spotless and the Holy Spirit is here to make sure that is done to the dot! When He appears you must be like Him. The Groom is coming, the Bride must be prepared. **The Holy Spirit is the spirit of preparation. He is, if you like, the Advance Party.**

> 2 Corinthians 3:18 *And all of us, as with unveiled face, [because we] continued to behold [in the Word of God] as in a mirror the glory of the Lord, are constantly being transfigured into His very own image in ever increasing splendor and from one degree of glory to another; [for this comes] from the Lord [Who is] the Spirit. (Amp)*

> Ephesians 4:15 *But speaking the truth in love, may grow up into him in all things, which is the head, even Christ…*

Scripture does not say **GROW IN HIM**, but grow **INTO HIM**. There is a difference. A very big one. You are being turned into the very likeness of Jesus. Can it be plainer than this? We are turning into His very image. **God is taking us to live with Him as Christ!** When

God looks at you and looks at Christ there is no difference for you have become Christ. *Sit down digest it slowly. We are coming to this point. But have you* **realized that the Mark of Christ is a spirit?** *Now that is a very important and dangerous point. Why? Because the mark is INVISIBLE! It is enshrined in character.* Friend, may the Lord Jesus open your eyes so that you escape what is before us. Am not scaring you, but pointing you to Him who is able to keep you in these times. What is so interesting is that when you accept Jesus in your life you are totally a new creature. John 3:6 tells us that when you are born again you become spirit. For you are born of the Spirit. And your position is with Christ on His Father's Throne. You sit in that throne. Revelation 3:21. The devil's child has also been given his father's throne. He, together with all who are his will rule from the devil's throne. **Know this: when you are in Christ you are in God. When you are in the Antichrist, you have received the mark, you are in the...? (Homework).**

The Mark Of The Beast

Just as the Christian mark is a spirit even the Antichrist's mark is a spirit! It is invisible. And it is not coming in ten years time.

> 1 John 4:3 *but every spirit that does not acknowledge Jesus is not from God. This is the spirit of the antichrist, which you have heard is coming and even now is already in the world. (NIV)*

So the spirit of the Antichrist is already here. It does not say *spirit of antichrist*, but **the spirit of the antichrist.** The spirit of the antichrist is the opposite of the spirit of Christ who is the Holy Spirit. The Bible calls the Holy Spirit the Spirit of Christ. But do you know what the spirit of the antichrist is doing? He is already in the world. Which world? The world system. And look at this

> Ephesians 2:2 *Wherein in time past ye walked according to the course of this world, according to the prince of the power of the air, the spirit that now worketh in the children of disobedience*

You walked according to the **course** of this **world**. That **course** is what we call **the system**. And we see that **the prince of the** power of the air is **the spirit working right now in the children of lawlessness! Without sounding offensive I would like to state that some people are truly the devil's children. And they are about their father's business.**

Purpose

Purpose is the key to unlocking what is before us. To what purpose is this wickedness? **The Antichrist spirit is here to change you into the image or nature or character of the Antichrist.** Every day you change more and more into his likeness. Every day just as Christians are moving from one degree of glory to another and becoming Christ, these are also moving from one degree of wickedness to another becoming Antichrist. **People are going to hell as the devil!** They are not going to hell because they are sinning. No. **They are going to Hell because they have become sin!** They are one, totally united with the devil. In Ephesians 4:15 Christians are growing INTO Christ. In a similar manner, the opposite is true. Friend I want you to know this, the mark of the Beast has two dimensions or sides. **It is both spiritual and physical.** In this case the spiritual or invisible precedes the physical. **It all starts in the spirit and culminates in the physical.** Many are running around in total fear that they may be branded by the antichrist without their knowledge. Come on child that is imagination running abnormally wild. In the midst of every problem or challenge there is good news. It is **IMPOSSIBLE** for you to receive the mark of the Beast. *Impossible. How?* **You can never receive the mark by accident.** You must consent. **The mark—the physical mark is given only to those who have the devil's disposition already in them.** Check this

> Romans 8:9 *But ye are not in the flesh, but in the Spirit, if so be that the Spirit of God dwell in you. Now if any man have not the Spirit of Christ, he is none of his.*

The opposite is true. If you do not have the spirit of the Antichrist you are none of his! You can only receive the physical mark when the spiritual is already at work. **You can tell if you are a candidate of this mark**

right now. The most dangerous is the spiritual, the invisible mark, the character. **People are turning into the devil.** And they do not know it? They do. If you like worrying, worry about the spiritual, not the physical, whose character do you exude?

> Galatians 4:19 *My little children, of whom I travail in birth again until Christ be formed in you*

My prayer is that the one who is being formed in you is Christ not the Antichrist! All those who worship the Antichrist, who have his nature will hate you very much. Friend when you talk about the mark of the Beast you are talking about his character, the character of the devil. (We are soon going to have a serious, full-fledged collision of anointings. For a long time this mysterious prophecy of Beasts arising has astounded generations. It seems to fit many eras. **Signs of fulfillment can be pin—pointed in history without any debate arising.** However certain details have not fitted in, they have not taken place. **Those details are just about to fit in now. This prophecy will not just go on it has to come to its total fulfillment and we are about to hit the inevitable Conclusion.** This is why greater attention has to be paid to the issues at hand. The details that fit the big picture. Live ready). What are the characteristics of this spirit which people are receiving?

Characteristics

> Galatians 5:19 *Now the doings (practices) of the flesh are clear (obvious): they are immorality, impurity, indecency,* 20 *Idolatry, sorcery, enmity, strife, jealousy, anger (ill temper), selfishness, divisions (dissensions), party spirit (factions, sects with peculiar opinions, heresies),* 21 *Envy, drunkenness, carousing, and the like. I warn you beforehand, just as I did previously, that those who do such things shall not inherit the kingdom of God.*

But are not those the normal qualities of the flesh? I mean weaknesses of the flesh? No dear. When God created man there were no weaknesses of the flesh. The weaknesses you are talking about came from Satan. That is why Jesus came. To completely destroy the Adamic nature that housed sin. The Adamic nature that Satan had dominion over, that was in the image of Satan, was removed from the shelves of the world super markets 2000 + years ago. Expired. Some refuse to believe that Jesus came. They are even ridiculing Jesus. *Jesus is a myth. It is a bunch of lunatics who brought it up. He never came.* **But do you know why they are saying Jesus never came?** It is to prepare for the coming man of lawlessness. As far as they are concerned there has never been a world savior. There has never been a person who is supernatural. **There has never been one above all problems, so when the evil one emerges they will point to him as the only one to have ever come to sort man's problems.** But we are not short sighted. We are not ignorant. Jesus came. I know very well. I live with Him. I talk to Him every day. We are family. What are you going to tell me? Some people will agree that Jesus came. Those who say He did have this to say about Him. *Oh Jesus, the one who was having sex with Mary Magdalene? He is false. In fact, He planned some scheme with Judas. Judas and Jesus are buddies.* Hooray. And you see Christians running around like chickens without heads, panting,

'Pastor, they found Jesus with Mary Magdalene.'
'Where son?'
'Somewhere, there is evidence.'
'Evidence?'
'Yes. This will stumble many people. But we are already Christians we just continue huh?'

Easy Child, take it easy. My advice is simple. Go and join the devil. You are no good for Jesus. If the Holy Spirit and you have an intimate relationship, nothing of that sort will move you. **The problem with many Christians is that the Jesus they know is on paper. He is not real.** Others all they see is a helpless baby in a filthy manger. You got it all wrong. You depend so much on some fake people's testimonies that God has failed to give you your own. I hate to be this frank with you, but it must come out. Joining a Church does not make you a Christian. Tithing does not make you a Christian. Singing does not make you a Christian either. Some demons are better singers, but they are still demons. **Whatever you do will not make you a Christian unless you have the new birth.** Some people think 'Born again' is a particular denomination. **Whether you are SDA, Methodist, Roman Catholic, Pentecostal, Charismatic, Baptist etc you are not a Christian if you are not born again.** And if you are not, then you do not belong to the Church of Jesus. The true Church of Jesus is Universal and the Bible says He knows those who are His. That means He knows those who are not His too. If you are born again then you must surely have the Holy Spirit. When you are born again you recognize in word and deed the Lordship of Jesus. And His Spirit in you confirms you are His. But not only that. The Holy Spirit must lead you. I tell you in these last days you are going to need Him more than you would need an aqualung (oxygen tank) under water.

2 Timothy 3:1 *BUT UNDERSTAND this, that in the last days will come (set in) perilous times of great stress and trouble [hard to deal with and hard to bear].*

2 *For people will be lovers of self and [utterly] self-centered, lovers of money and aroused by an inordinate [greedy] desire for wealth, proud and arrogant and contemptuous boasters. They will be abusive (blasphemous, scoffing), disobedient to parents, ungrateful, unholy and profane.*

3 *[They will be] without natural [human] affection (callous and inhuman), relentless (admitting of no truce or appeasement); [they will be] slanderers (false accusers, troublemakers), intemperate and loose in morals and conduct, uncontrolled and fierce, haters of good.*

4 *[They will be] treacherous [betrayers], rash, [and] inflated with self-conceit. [They will be] lovers of sensual pleasures and vain amusements more than and rather than lovers of God.*

False prophets will come with some revelations. Christians are not supposed to be dull. A false prophet is not just a man or woman of the cloth. A false prophet is one who is professing what he or she does not even understand... He or she claims to have some hidden gems. A false prophet is one who is working under the spirit of the antichrist. A prophet, in the general sense of the word, is not just a religious person, but someone who has ideas he or she thinks the world should hear about. Certain topics are harmless, but others should make us put the spirituality of the 'prophet' in a test tube. We are told to test the spirit, for many false prophets are in the world...He could be a farmer, a banker, a university professor etc. One must know that the spirit of the antichrist is here for a reason.

Reason

One of the greatest things you must know is that the spirit of the antichrist is here so that he can present you to the Antichrist on that day when he appears without any Christian spots! **The spirit of the Antichrist is the spirit of preparation.** *That is why Christians must know what they know.* Some of these funny things that some of these boys and girls are running around trying to fool the masses with, we have seen them coming a long time ago. **They can yodel, jump, kill themselves, I know Jesus and I know what is going on.** I understand spiritual operations. And I say that with firmness and humility. I am not moved by their simple discoveries. I know what happens in the spirit world. I know how the devil feels about the Holy Spirit. I know how Jesus is reverenced. IF Jesus was false He wouldn't have the impact He carries. HELL literally freezes in His presence. I know this very well. And not from hearsay. Now this is what you should know.

The Mark:

What do we notice about the mark? **It is carried by followers.** There is no forcing on the receipt of the mark. The mark is received willingly. *Huh?* Yes.

> Revelation 13:3 *And one of his heads seemed to have a deadly wound.*
> *But his death stroke was healed; and the whole earth*
> *went after the beast in amazement and admiration.*
> 4 *They fell down and paid homage to the dragon,*
> *because he had bestowed on the*
> *beast all his dominion and authority; they*
> *also praised and worshiped the beast,*
> *exclaiming, Who is a match for the*

beast, and, Who can make
war against him?

Can you see it? No one has forced these people to fall before the beast. None. **They went after the** Beast in **Amazement** and **Admiration!** They want to be him!!! And because of this they **worship the Devil**. I remember evangelizing in Simoonga, a village on the outskirts of Livingstone in the mid 1990s. I found a paralytic. This woman had been to four witch doctors, but without any success. I told her that Jesus was able to change her life by healing her. I told her that what those four witch doctors could not do, Jesus could. I simply tapped on her knees and pulled her up. She walked instantly. I smiled with great satisfaction and told her sweetly to give her life to Jesus. She looked at me with her beautiful face and said, 'I can't.' There are shockwaves and there are **tsunamis**. I was experiencing the latter. She saw the horror and confusion on my face. She said, 'My husband will not accept the mention of the name of Jesus in his house, so I can't accept Jesus.' Fascinating. Even the other people present were tsunami*ed* with shock! **It is not true that the devil forces people always.** He is loved. I know you blinked and missed that. Read it again. In another incident somebody came home seeking help. I rushed to his house. When we got there he told me that he was having a lot of spiritual problems. **As we prayed together the Holy Spirit was urging me to ask for the meaning of his name**. (*I don't tell people to change names, but at this moment the Holy spirit was urging me to ask him the meaning of a certain name which I was hearing.*) When I asked about the name the Spirit of God was giving me he looked at me and said, 'That is the spirit that keeps me.' I told him that he wouldn't get deliverance if he did not get rid of the spirit. He told me that the spirit had been very good to him he could not get rid of it. **All he wanted from me was to** *just sort* **out his spiritual problems.** I left and never looked back. If you put Jesus here and the devil there and nicely and slowly explain the two persons before them and what they stand for. Guess what? After 100 million years of explaining some people will still choose the devil! They love what he stands for. These blind people worship the beast and his papa the dragon because they think he has power over death and because he puts to death all his opponents—the Christians. That is how much some fellas love you. They want you dead. Look carefully at the scripture why they worship the beast. **Not because**

he is good. They worship him because he is a bad guy. What people consider strength and what God regards as strength are very different. No wonder they think God's patience is folly. Let me assure you. You have all eternity to discover that. Compare this animal with our Master Jesus Christ.

Revelation 5:7 *He then went and took the scroll from the right hand of Him Who sat on the throne.*

8 *And when He had taken the scroll, the four living creatures and the twenty-four elders [of the heavenly Sanhedrin] prostrated themselves before the Lamb. Each was holding a harp (lute or guitar), and they had golden bowls full of incense (fragrant spices and gums for burning), which are the prayers of God's people (the saints).*

9 *And [now] they sing a new song, saying, You are worthy to take the scroll and to break the seals that are on it, for You were slain (sacrificed), and with Your blood You purchased men unto God from every tribe and language and people and nation.*

10 *And You have made them a kingdom (royal race) and priests to our God, and they shall reign [as kings] over the earth! Amp.*

The former is worshipped because he kills, the latter because he was killed to save His people. The former is visibly selfish the latter unselfish. Who do the masses pick?

People will follow the Antichrist willingly. This must help open our eyes. **Some people just love Satan and all he represents.** He is their father. **All Satan's children will follow their brother the Antichrist without any compulsion and compunction**. Most of the people will worship the image of the beast without the threat of death. In Revelation 13:16 the Bible says, 'He causeth…' The word **'causeth'** means the receiver has the option to consent or not. The whole idea is to make you **transgress the law.** He wants you to **'yield.'** And if you look at the word for **'receive'** in the same verse it means

- **To Give**
- **To Grant**
- **To Bestow**

- **To Number**

The recipient is in one way or the other responsible. And what is even more interesting is that the word **'receive'** in Revelation 14:11, 19:20 and 20:4 means *to take or accept out of amazement or interest!* They **wondered** after the Beast, remember? It also means **to lay hold of. There is determination to get this, to have it!** How many of the devil's delicacies are we gulping in the name of modernization and moderation? Plenty. Is the devil pulling us by the hands? No, in fact we remind him to supply us with more. He is failing to keep up with our pace. The mark of the beast is an honor for some to have that's why it is **BESTOWED!** It is **conferred**, are you getting this? (Do you remember Ezekiel 9:4?) What is inside is what determines your receiving the mark. The mark is the nature or character of the beast. **The mark is the spirit from the pit of hell.** What are we saying then? **The first part of giving the mark of the beast is already at work, but this is not the final.** At this moment you can walk away on the devil. **But when the second dimension, the physical is introduced and you receive it, there is no going back. You are doomed. Eternally.** People will receive the mark of the beast with great pride. It is an honour. And we see that the masses love and even admire the man of sin. They want to be him! Selfishness and not love and faithfulness are the driving force of the wicked. The level of people getting into the kingdom of darkness in one way or the other is so appalling. There is no community that has been spared. Demonic hordes have been released and are causing destruction. **But it must be pointed out that these demons that are operating here are operating legally!**

Legally? *Keyworth that's preposterous.* It isn't. Demons are here because they have been called through prayer. Right now some people are carrying out prayers for the devil to release those demons that will carry out the devil's latest strategy. Both long term and short term. **To rule the world using a man has been the devil's greatest assignment.** And he is not about to relent. If you will be lazy in your prayers the Satanists are not. Satan worship is both individual and collective. Much havoc has been done on individual basis. World catastrophes take collective prayers and assignments. As spirit beings Satanists travel out of their bodies and can cause much destruction which some wise people will wisely ascribe to 'mother nature'. As people start playing with one form of witchcraft or the other for example, to get promotion on a job, to get a particular woman or man, for their business to thrive etc, what they do not know is that they are enlisting into the devil's kingdom. The devil will always make things tough and he wants you to go to him for a solution. What you are joining is not innocent. You will pay dearly. This abnormal desire to turn against God and do things clandestinely is part of this antichrist spirit. We are not saying everything that goes wrong in the world is done by Satanists, no. But the implementation of many EVIL schemes that are causing untold pain or suffering is surely theirs'. I know this beyond **a billion percent certainty!**

Enlisting is easy, but try coming out and you will know what I am blabbing about. The decision is entirely up to you. The one you love is the one you will follow. If the devil is good, throw Jesus away. Why bother? If Jesus is good kick the devil out, but you can't have both.

B. False Prophet's Police 9

Revelation 13:17 *and that no man might buy or sell, save he that had the... the name of the beast*

For a long time now the clergy have been at pains trying to make people understand the greatness of the Name of Jesus. *Command in Jesus Name. Do this in Jesus' name.* When you are given the name (in this case the Name of Jesus it means you have become one). The people of old—Israelites and non Israelites understood this clearly Deuteronomy 28:10. *Why don't we?* When you are called by His Name you carry Him. All the time. Jesus is the final name. Use it. It has all power. You must be a strange Christian to speak the Name of Jesus without impact. The Name of Jesus is supernatural. **Where it is mentioned there is power and a change in circumstance.** That Name always carries miracles with it. . *Well, here is the wake up call. The devil is coming for practicals. And he is not playing games.* He is coming with a name too.

After the mark has been given there are some who will ascend the ladder, the law enforcers. All law enforcers will do it in the Name of the Beast—the supposed lord of the universe. There are certain things we do in the name of the President of the country. When the world ruler comes things will be done in his name too! But the level will be very high. **The name is associated with power or law enforcement.** What did Jesus say?

Matthew 28:18 *And Jesus coming up spoke to*

them, saying, All power has been
given me in heaven and
upon earth.

Jesus commissioned his disciples to go and make disciples of all nations. But we must not forget we are doing it in **His Name**. Why? He is the **Authority**. Now this must open some believers' eyes. **You are the law enforcer when you use the name of Jesus. You are the spiritual police.** What you say stands! It is because some people understand who they are that's why they are called 'name and claim it'. Call them names they know what they are doing and you don't. Sometimes we oppose things out of maximum ignorance.

Acts 4:10 *Let it be known and understood by all of you, and by the whole house of Israel, that in the name and through the power and authority of Jesus Christ of Nazareth, Whom you crucified, [but] Whom God raised from the dead, in Him and by means of Him this man is standing here before you well and sound in body.*

11 *This [Jesus] is the Stone which was despised and rejected by you, the builders, but which has become the Head of the corner [the Cornerstone].*

12 *And there is salvation in and through no one else, for there is no other name under heaven given among men by and in which we must be saved.*

L*et it be known to all of you Christians that there is only one lord of the universe and it is …*This scripture is going to be directly challenged and changed. The Bible publicly outlawed because it claims there is another name above the name of the Antichrist. This is directly against the world constitution. World constitution? *Keyworth I know you have gone overboard but world constitution? You have lost it completely.* How I wish I had Dear. Yes there is a world constitution around the corner. Just a few more steps and you do not have to worry whether I am bluffing or not. The world court will declare you villain number one. Sounds farfetched. *May I be allowed to make it worse?* The preparation for this has already been done.

Soon the Name of Jesus is going to be a direct threat to the world. And to the new world ruler. That is why the system has to get rid of anything with the badge of Jesus. What will happen to us? *We shall flee* *into the bush.* Carry enough food we are going into the bush! Wonderful idea. Great thinking. We have seen Hollywood films of people running away from the Antichrist, living in the bush.

Entertainment or education? I believe the producers and actors of these films mean well to warn the masses what lies in the not so distant future. God bless them. But many forget one important factor. **We ain't gonna run.** It is head on. The system has been put in place so that you cannot hide even if you ran. You will have to choose between the Antichrist and Jesus. Jesus is not interested in you running away either. He is interested in the answer you are going to give the Antichrist. Your answer is what determines whether you are a Christian or not. **Revelation 13:10. Don't look it up. You won't like what it says. But that is the acid test. Our sufficiency is from Him.** Two things are going to come out of you when you are squeezed.

Patience and faith. Many will be put to the sword. Now being put to the sword Allan does not mean 'sword', the big knife. You will be tortured with the various advanced demonic techniques so that you breakdown. But one thing I know, you are not the kind that breaks down before the enemy.

Read my book **'Though The Waters…Roar —Undiluted Faith.' No matter what comes your way, you do not breakdown before your enemy. That's the God Standard. Listen, there is a big difference between crying and breaking down. Jesus cried, but He never broke down!** In the same scripture, Revelation 13:10 God warns anyone who harms His saints. He promises them tit for tat. How wonderful.

Oh no Pastor you have mixed it up. We are not going to be here. Thank you sir. I am not talking about millennialism or amillennialism we have all eternity to talk about that over a cup of coffee in Heaven, my concern is this, my friend, **live ready**. Some things are already happening right now, and it is time to have a stance. Don't be a coward. Heaven can wait. The world needs your undying loyalty to Jesus today. Demonstrate it.

People around you are beginning to say the Antichrist is the law. Yes by their character they are admitting he is the law therefore he must be followed. What do you think people are saying when they chant 'New World Order'? What spirit is behind?

How many things today carry the label of New World Order? *The American dollar.* Yes Jane, but that is the lighter side. It's not just our government policies but our education and social systems. **Do you know the source of the things you sheepishly follow?** Jesus is folding His hands and watching. Is your faith going to overcome? What we see, the physical is temporal. What is spiritual is permanent. You catch the spiritual by faith, with your spirit. Put your all on Jesus! Count on the integrity of His Word.

Ever been faced with a storm, all the signs show you are sinking, but Jesus says **you are not?** Friend cast your all on Jesus. **Character, like bread is baked in an oven.** The dough undergoes intense heat, but when it is all over the scent that wafts from it will water every mouth. Mouths will literally drool; pools of saliva will be created. That is why we need those who have been 'through it,' not wishful thinkers. There are some means God may use to develop your character, they are not good in the short term, trust me, I know what am talking about. But it is wonderful later when you stand on the summit, unmoved by anything. Mature.

The system is in place even in leadership. We must be firm. The Bible is very clear on the world leadership. There are three kinds of political leaders.

- Those who do everything possible to ascend to the throne Hosea 8:4
- Those who are wicked and are the devil's messengers Psalm 2
- And those who are God's ministers and He has let them ascend to the throne Romans 13: 1–8.

'Satan's Best Kept Secrets' is my next book and in it I explain in detail the three kingdoms. Out of the three kingdoms, two of them are supernatural. And both have sent ambassadors to control the earth. But the devil's ambassadors are going to have more control of this place more than God's people. *What? The devil is more powerful than God?* I didn't say that Kenny. The devil's people are going to have more control over this earth.

> Psalm 2:1 *Why do the nations conspire and the peoples plot in vain?* [2] *The kings of the earth take their stand and the rulers gather together against the* LORD *and against his Anointed One.* [3] *"Let us break their chains," they say, "and throw off their fetters."*
> *(NIV)*

Presidents and some influential people in the world will conspire against God and Christ and do everything possible to destroy Christianity. We are seeing some things being put in place that are totally against Christ. Is this sinking in you? These Presidents who will be under demonic influence will override what God fearing Presidents will do.

Other influential men and women who fear God will be sidelined too. Their inputs or efforts will be thwarted. It should also be noted that there would be an International uprising against Christianity. This is towards the rise of the wicked one just as he is about to come. When he comes the Bible says presidents will hand over their power to him and this is the fella whose prophet will unleash his police on you. (Now you understand where these regional integrations are taking us to. They look good and sound sensible, but behind all this effort to stabilize our economies and make a better life is the rise of the worst person since creation—the devil's first son.) There is going to be a new Interpol. An Interpol meant for you and me dear. And they will come in the name of the unquestionable, the lord of the universe the immortal one, god of all, the Antichrist. (John I did not mean his name is going to be called Antichrist no, no, no. He will have a sweet name like any other person. But his character is to come as an imposter and while pretending to be the real Christ he will try to undo all that Jesus the true Christ has done. Call him a mole if you like, but a damned one). The nations will be very very angry against God and Jesus that they will desire to destroy whatever connects them to God and Christ. And do you know what that bond is? You, me and the Bible. We are the ones to reinforce the

Lordship of Jesus here. We are the bonds who are teaching His Word to the world.

Law enforcers will move in without the slightest iota of mercy, after all, they would have already received the mark themselves—the character of the antichrist. My dear it is not an easy issue. But I want you to understand this. Right now things are going on. Things have been put in place to capture all who will **Not Worship** the Antichrist. '*Me I am not the religious sort,*' some say. Who is? That won't protect you from what has come! This conspiracy has been going on insidiously. **This is the mystery of Lawlessness. As they dismantle all that God is doing in our lives they will be introducing something from the pit of hell.** For every Word of God thrown out, there is a demonic one put on the world shelves for people to purchase.

It must not come as a strange thing for people to come up with things 'better' than the Bible. *Who wants to follow some outdated rumblings of mad men? The Bible is fiction at the highest level.* **Son, I couldn't agree with you more.** Only problem, those rumblings of madmen are proving very sane. You do not have to argue with the Bible especially today. It's dead accurate!

Could you simply ask God if He is really God to open your eyes and carry out your research about the things the Bible talks about and the things that have been put down in this book? Son, your jaw won't plop, it will sublime! That is why **tolerance**, **fellowships** and **moderation** are becoming sweet words now. Their master fears the Bible. There is something supernatural about it. Moderation is being advocated more than ever before. The truth is Christians have always been tolerant. The devil has sown a few tares and we are being judged by the standard of these tares. Believe it or not the Bible is going to be outlawed. When this happens you and I will have to face one truth, we can never, no matter what, turn away from Jesus. We will be hunted down like animals.

Matthew 24:9 *Then shall they deliver you up to be*
afflicted, and shall kill you: and ye
shall be hated of all nations
for my name's
sake.

Why shall you be hated by ALL the NATIONS? **His Name's sake!!!!!** The Name is everything. This is reality. This is happening. Clandestine meetings are going on right now at different levels to put all this into force. **The Name of Jesus, what a Name! Many will lose lives just for this Name. Is it worth it? Is this Name worth losing your life for?**

Eddie it is an honor only few are accorded. May you never shrink back if the Lord accords you this rare opportunity.

> Acts 5:41 *And they departed from the presence of the council, rejoicing that they were counted worthy to suffer shame for his name.*

Such times we may have nothing left, for even the little property we owned could remain in other people's hands. Let us fully understand we are pilgrims. This is one time we must come face to face with this reality. We are International Criminals. Rebels. But we are fearless. Not even death is a problem. Courage runs in our veins…

C. False Prophet's Priests 10

Mark 3:6 and the pharisees went forth, and straightway took counsel with the herodians against him, How they might destroy him.

False prophets are already going about their master's business, but the one who surpasses them all is around the bend.

A lot of things could be mentioned about the false prophets and their workmanship. But three things stand out. These are the things that characterized the religious archenemies of Jesus the Pharisees. From Mark 2:22–3:6 we see three characteristics of the Pharisees.

(i)Full Of Religious Pride: Gods

They looked outwardly clean. In the market places they were given the greatest of greetings because of the pomp with which they carried themselves. Greeting one of them would make you feel blessed for the rest of that decade. The phylacteries they displayed amplified it all. *Who wouldn't be moved?* These were the 'gods'. Unerring. They seemed to have been keeping the law to the letter. None could fault them until Jesus put them in His spiritual lab and found gangrene and cancer in their system.

Lawyers and others teamed up to finish the Galilean off. But they were in for a great rude awakening. Jesus was no ordinary Galilean.

(ii)Fault Finders: Attack The Good

They knew Jesus was good, he was clean, but he did not give them the 'reverence' they craved because he knew them.

So they looked at His life critically. Every time Jesus did something that they were not pleased with they pulled a few strings and the next day the headlines were unkind:

"JESUS THE TRUE MESSIAH BLUNDERS"

"JESUS TALKS MORE THAN 'KINDLY' TO A WOMAN AT A WELL"

"JESUS IS CARESSED IN PUBLIC BY A PROSTITUTE"

"JESUS FALLS FOR ZACHEAUS' RICHES"

"PRIDE OR POWER? Jesus To Rebuild Temple In 72 Hours!"

If there was anyone who knew what Jesus was all about it were the Pharisees. But their hearts were hardened against the truth. They loved darkness.

(iii)Friends Of The World

Envenomed with all that hell could provide they took it to the next level, they went political. They did not want to leave Jesus alone. This was more than personal. If Jesus had companies they would have tried to squeeze them using some special taxes or IRS arrangements. We call that 'Government Machinery'. Capitulate or else…One thing was very clear about the Pharisees they knew very well they were super hypocrites.

Personal gain stood at the center of all they did. And the people were theirs; no one had the right to talk to them in another way especially one they did not approve of. While they talked about God who judges the wicked, they did not waste time to carry out their own judgement. They were the jury, judges and executioners, no wonder Jesus told them they were gods in John 10:34. Within a few split seconds they found him guilty and were ready to slaughter him. **As we embrace**

the New Word Disorder, our new found light, we are going to see familiar characteristics. Mistakes of the true children of God will be amplified and the wickedness of the devil's puppies swept under the carpet.

Remote voices will be heard. A few voices will try to scream this and that, but who cares? They may scream this but no one will pay attention. The truth has no room. *We have heard that one before we want something new.* And God in heaven says thank you, new you will get. *Isn't Dad fair? God is fair.*

Offence is not in their gospel. It is all embracing. It is neutral. We do not need to be contentious we are all one, the Gospel of Jesus is love and peace. Come on dear, the gospel is offensive. **Explain it in blue and green, black and white, jump, howl, scream you will come to one true conclusion: the gospel is offensive.** As you share it in love and with a blessed face like yours dear, somebody somewhere will rise in total anger. These don't need anger management, it won't work. The same gospel is their cure. The devil is trying to cut the supply of medicine to the patients. James, we do not relent, do we? Nay.

Perhaps this is where we move another step to finding out the third thing, The Number 666. Many books have been written about 666. I won't dwell on the value or the meaning of the number 666. I would like us to look at this from a slightly different angle. The meaning of **'To number'.** To number comes from the Old Testament.

> Numbers 4:23 *From thirty years old and upward until fifty years old shalt thou number them; all that enter in to perform the service, to do the work in the tabernacle of the congregation.*

I strongly believe **'numbering'** directly affects the **'priests'** or clergy. **They are the key factor for the next world set up.** A careful study of this scripture, reveals that the priests are actually leading people into **spiritual warfare** through their work in the tabernacle! The words **perform** and **service** are words for spiritual warfare! (THESE TWO WORDS MEAN PREPARING AN ARMY FOR WAR! If only we knew this. That's why they want to water down the importance of the Church. They know it is war. Do we?) The false prophet will also do the same. He will enlist them to stand against Jesus Christ! It is important to understand the various words that are used in 'to number'. But the prominent one is the Hebrew **'Paqad.'** That is the word used in the above scripture. And looking up the Greek word 'Airo' from which arithmos comes and its Hebrew counterpart 'Nasa' we see various meanings of 'to number'. Here are some meanings.

- **To visit with friendly intent e.g. Genesis 21:1**
- **To appoint to have the charge e.g. Judges 21:9**
- **To visit with hostile intent e.g. 1 Samuel 2:21**

And from the word were 'arithmos'(this is the word used in Revelation) is derived we get

- **To forgive**
- **To make to doubt**.

The characteristics of the number 666 are enshrined in those definitions. Whatever his name is, at least some things are clear, the **underlying character is revealed in those definitions.**

a) To visit with friendly intent e.g. Genesis 21:1

Putting the various words for number together we see that the false prophet— 'numbers' i.e. paying God's children, specifically the ministers of the Gospel a visit, with friendly or hostile intent. Meaning he comes with a proposal. You and I are not new to Satan's proposals. You get a raw deal, always. It is his style. He comes to you and he proposes a nice talk over a cup of coffee. Beware. You cannot move from being God's priest to being the devil's priest. That is beyond sinking low!

b) To appoint to have the charge e.g. Judges 21:9

He shows you a way. A way that exalts you. **A way that 'numbers'— exalts self.** Pride is at the centre of the coming world religious system. Friend we are back to Eden. **No matter how high a position the devil**

can offer you it will always not be above your sole. For the devil will always be under your feet. Don't aim to fail. Aim high, where Jesus is.

Genesis 3:1 *NOW THE serpent was more subtle and crafty than any living creature of the field which the Lord God had made. And he [Satan] said to the woman, Can it really be that God has said, You shall not eat from every tree of the garden?*

2 *And the woman said to the serpent, We may eat the fruit from the trees of the garden,*

3 *Except the fruit from the tree which is in the middle of the garden. God has said, You shall not eat of it, neither shall you touch it, lest you die.*

4 *But the serpent said to the woman, You shall not surely die,*

5 *For God knows that in the day you eat of it your eyes will be opened, and you will be like God, knowing the difference between good and evil and blessing and calamity.*

6 *And when the woman saw that the tree was good (suitable, pleasant) for food and that it was delightful to look at, and a tree to be desired in order to make one wise, she took of its fruit and ate; and she gave some also to her husband...*

c) To make to doubt

He *numbers* you—**makes you doubt**.

Eve's sin was doubt. She doubted the character of God. Satan told her God was a crook who did not want them to be as great as He is. The devil's boy will deceive many. Some will move in power—miraculous power and think they are invincible.

d) To forgive

The other meaning for the word number is 'forgive'. After making you doubt that you were on the right course he will forgive or pardon your ignorance. The lord of the universe, god himself will forgive your sins. Sounds farfetched? I really wish. The Antichrist is coming as god. Remember nobody since the world began has ever lied like these two guys. I know you have met liars, but those will kick their legs in repentance that they do not know what lying is. This guy has perfected the art. With a smooth face and a smooth tongue he lies his way to your heart and captures it. Many will see sense in what will be told them. They will see light. **But not all light is light.**

Some light carries darkness. And why should you be **forgiven**? Because you have sinned against the **only** God—the Antichrist. He does not stop at forgiving you. He appoints you to a place of **exaltation**.

Daniel 11:32 *And such as violate the covenant*
he shall pervert and seduce
with flatteries

Look at the key words there. He shall **pervert** and **seduce** with **flatteries**. *Oh God. Who doesn't want to be flattered? Pastor you are the best preacher, you are the best.* And your heart races like a formula one car. But the fella does not even mean it. Flattery. This boy who is coming has perfected this art. He is a terrible liar. And he's supposed to be the savior of the world? Believe it or not, the higher one goes in Satanic activities the lowest the integrity becomes, but what do the masses say? *That's our man*. Thank you. Your man, not mine. Jesus is my man. **The Bible says what people respect very much is what is an abomination to God**. Luke 16:15. What a Word! After this liar has cooked up nice stories he does something to the religious people. What does he make them?

Priest–kings. These are the temporal priest–kings of the world.

2Corinthians 4:18 *Since we consider and look not to the things*
that are seen but to the things that are unseen; for
the things that are visible are temporal (brief
and fleeting), but the things that are
invisible are deathless and
everlasting. (Amp)

Revelation 1:6 *and He has made us to be a kingdom,*
priests to His God and Father—to Him be
the glory and the dominion forever
and ever. Amen.

10 *"You have made them to be a kingdom and priests to our God; and they will reign upon the earth."*

The opposite is what many want. These are the people who assist the false prophet in services of worship as priests in the demonic kingdom. If you really look at some of the hierarchy in the kingdom of darkness you will realize that they have titles of **kings** and **priests**! (Besides they have **spiritual books** they follow. It's actually a **'church.'** So let no one fool you with '*this church stuff*,' they are in the devil's camp! The things we tell people that they exist, that day they will see with their eye balls without the help of contact lenses.) That is what it means to number. **Enlisted into the priesthood of darkness.** It is being 'numbered'—married to the Antichrist. This is meant for those who are in ministry those who have the offices. If you are part of the clergy this is your part—this is what the false prophet has for you. **He puts you on the antichrists' pay roll with all the goodies to spoil you.** Believe me it will seem like forever as you enjoy those demonic delicacies when suddenly in a trice all the quick sands you depended on begin to reveal their shifting nature. Plop you go with the wicked ones.

Remember this guy is coming as god. 2 Thessalonians 2:4. **The next world ruler is coming as King.** The next world ruler can never be a president. **He is a god**. He could start as a president but it has to come to one point, he is god. This is why one has to be very careful when people talk about 'being gods.' **There is a fissure.** There are those who are saying it from the Antichrist's point of view! Before the main god comes his little ones are already moving around chanting 'gods'. Careful. And this god who is coming does not believe in you having any freedom or independent thinking. Bow before him without any question. Please be careful with any leader who attains the level of being unquestionable. Secret societies are keeping most of their business a secret, because if you knew, your heart would sink. **And you will be shocked how they are using democracy to bring about untold evil.** *Keyworth, are you saying democracy is being used to bring about the rise of the antichrist from the religious angle?* Good student. Correct. Democracy has been used at *higher religious* levels to bring unbelievable bloodshed in the past and currently.

If you carefully look at what is being put across by the false prophet this is what Jesus has already offered us. Look at all the points and meanings of 'to number'. It is what Christ has already offered. But ignorance will make one worship a dog to get a loaf of bread. **What Satan is offering through his child is a poor imitation of what Christ has already offered.** It is a curse not to live life in the Holy Spirit. You cannot constantly reject Him and get away with it. Satan will get you. The Spirit of God lets you understand spiritual issues. There is just a lot more than your eye balls can see. And there is a lot more than death. Refuse to be cursed. Bowing before the devil makes you cursed.

Proverbs 3:33 *The curse of the LORD is in the house of the wicked: but he blesseth the habitation of the just.*

Where is the curse of the Lord? In the house of the wicked. The devil is the wicked one and all his children are cursed. Do not allow the curse of the Antichrist to fall upon you. He is cursed and you are not.

Embarking on this evil way of life may seem joyous but very terrible in the end. Many are doing that. One thing we cannot fail to point out about this man is this: **He is a prophet**. But a false one. And since he is a prophet what does he do? Thank you Bob, he can **predict** the future and it comes to pass just like that! That is the most dangerous characteristic of this fella. He performs miracles not only calling fire down but he has the ability to perform miracles of foretelling. And all the worship and prophecies will be done in the name of the Antichrist, the god of the universe.

Seems bleak for us huh? Never. Not even a bit. Let me reveal to you the secret of persecution that many do not really see. Jesus experienced the same thing. It is not easy, but this is when faith is put to the ultimate test. It is time we let go of this faith of believing Jesus for a loaf of bread, a huge bank account to the point where we believe Him for our very lives. We must, like the Lord Jesus say **Into Your Hands I commend my spirit.** That my friend is Undiluted faith. Here it is.

John 19:10 *Then saith Pilate unto him, Speakest thou not unto me? knowest thou not that I have power to crucify thee, and have power to release thee?* [11] *Jesus answered, Thou couldest have no power at all against me, except it were given thee from above: therefore he that delivered me unto thee hath the greater sin.*

Pilate does not have power to crucify you. Do you see that? God has just allowed it.

This is something you must comprehend. The devil is not in charge. The Kingdom or Throne of God is above all kingdoms. Psalm 103:19. Nobody is above your Daddy. Always judge things from their spiritual perspective. What many do not know is that even the Antichrist himself will just be **'allowed'** to do his thing, but he is a fly that is approaching a volcano!

Smile we are never outnumbered or outwitted. That you can bet your life on! You may be treated as a fugitive for a few days but soon you will rule over all those who had the short lived reign. Be prayerful and may the living God keep you according to His Word

John 10:29 *My Father, which gave them me, is greater than all; and no man is able to pluck them out of my Father's hand.*

You are in Safe Hands. In God the Father of our Lord Jesus' Hands nobody can pluck you. Believe me, **nobody!**

IV. Characteristics Of The Mark

Romans 1:28 And even as they did not like to retain God in their knowledge, God gave them over to a reprobate mind, to do those things which are not convenient; 29 Being filled with all unrighteousness, fornication, wickedness, covetousness, maliciousness; full of envy, murder, debate, deceit, malignity; whisperers, 30 Backbiters, haters of God, despiteful, proud, boasters, inventors of evil things, disobedient to parents, 31 Without understanding, covenant breakers, without natural affection, implacable, unmerciful…

A. Freedom Unlimited 11

Isaiah 5:20 Woe unto them that call evil good, and good evil;
that put darkness for light, and light for darkness;
that put bitter for sweet, and sweet for bitter!
21 Woe unto them that are wise in their own
eyes, and prudent in their
own sight!

'Freedom! Freedom! Freedom! Everyone is chanting. What freedom are you talking about?'

'Freedom to be my own boss.'

'What are you talking about child? Do you know what you are saying?'

'Yes!'

'Freedom to do whatever you feel like?'

'Yeah. As a Christian I have the right. I can do whatever I feel like doing, Jesus died for me.'

'I sure do agree with you. You are free indeed. After all whom the Son sets free is free indeed.'

'No matter how much I sin the blood of Jesus still cleanses me.'

'I am not sure I still follow your line of thinking. Are you saying it doesn't matter how you live after getting saved?'

'Yeah it no matters not.'

'Child you have completely lost it. There is no freedom to sin like a maniac in God's kingdom. You can't be your own boss. Jesus paid the price for you.'

'Yes but Jesus died for the spirit, right?'

Reality check tells you that is wrong thinking. The body is important. The body is God's dwelling place, so you should know how to behave in the presence of The Almighty.

1Corinthians 6:19 *What? know ye not that your body is the temple of the Holy Ghost which is in you, which ye have of God, and ye are not your own?*

Entertaining false gospels at Jesus expense will not make you great, but make you regret. All the hocus–pocus of threading strange teachings to impress those with itching ears will land many into serious problems. Stop short circuiting the gospel for personal gain. Jesus will not take it kindly. **If you want to sin go and do it, but don't do it in the name of the gospel. You will compound your misery.**

Deuteronomy 5:11 *Thou shalt not take the name of the LORD thy God in vain: for the LORD will not hold him guiltless that taketh his name in vain.*

We have seen the rise of false family patterns, gay marriages. Uncommitted spouses who are always a.w.o.l. They do not care about anyone, after all they are their own boss. *'Christianity is restricting,'* they belch. **I agree with you. Christianity is very restricting, why entangle yourself with such misery when you can have joie de vivre outside Christianity? I am sure Christians must be blockheads, why couldn't they come up with ingenious thinking like yours?** Freedom of life, you are your own boss. That's new religion. New World Disorder—The Grand Rebellion. The missing link? The leader of the rebellion—son of darkness. And he's just about to join the fray.

Enjoy while you can. Children are now parents, they have rights to puke anything in the faces of parents. Yeah take your parents to police. Suddenly everyone has a story to tell and it is **abuse, abuse, abuse, abuse. Parents are living in corners dreading their kids.** Come on, what nonsense is this? Am I trivializing the abuse that is going on? No. Not even for a second. My heart bleeds. My heart goes to both the victims and perpetrators. Perpetrators? Yes. They are flies caught in a huge death web, and they do not understand some things they do. Some of them. But we must understand, the roots of some of these things. The spirit behind. Abuse is real, but…**It is exaggerated. Highly amplified. And it is manipulative. It is a license to justify the squashing of God's standard for the family.** Rights? From whom? Yes there are so many issues affecting people. I agree with rights up to a certain level. After that I know people are being pushed to cross the line by the kingdom of darkness. Families are disintegrating. And many of our policy makers are encouraging what is going on. I can't blame them, in fact I congratulate them. Romans 1:32. **At least they have the sense to be loyal to their master.** We don't. Most of us we just parrot what they tell us. Somebody somewhere brings in a replacement for the Bible and when that is effected, people become less alert, the devil unleashes demonic forces that find no resistance on their way. The result? The anarchy we see. Their next stage? Introduce the rights. We cannot be fooled. We are not ignorant of the devil's devices or tricks. **Cheap tricks**.

Demons are running the show and we seem to be mesmerized. The devil has come up with a very sweet religion. He knows how man behaves. He is introducing a sophisticated religion. **It does not tell you, 'Come and bow before this altar.' No. It says you can be your own boss**.

'Alas. Are you sure devil you mean that?'

'More than sure,' he hisses *'I swear upon my auntie'*. **Be your own boss.** With that many enlist. But what has never been revealed to them is that there is nothing like being your own boss. Being your own boss is what made the great Lucifer become Satan, the devil. The grand rebellion we are seeing will culminate in shocking disappointment. You will realize what a guinea pig you were when the waters reach your nose.

Not only will the water reach your nostrils it will be boiling. Problems compounded. Heartache.

One must not take this lightly. You do not have many chances. This is your only time and you had better not waste it. The worst thing to ever happen to any person is not death, but regret. Regret always means you wish things would be undone. Today is the moment you can undo, tomorrow is not guaranteed.

May you never regret your time on earth. It is painful to waste your life over something that does not last. Something that does not profit. Be wise.

Until we realize there are false brethren among us, brethren who were predicted in the Old Testament, who will do what their father does best, come as angels of light and begin to call the shots, we will not be effective. When they come they will try to dilute our faith. **They are sent with the weapon of flattery.** Flattery looks simple but it is a great demonic tool. Friend it is time. **Contend for the faith**. You don't contend without opposition. Jude recognizes this group and gives details of their character. It is time for the whole body of Christ to arise. It is time we were known as the greatest force in the universe—The Body of the Almighty.

Not sissy Christianity. Some unbiblical things are taking place in the Church. People are coming to Church to see the pastor perform then go home. Hooray. Christianity is over. *Our pastor prays.* Good. And what do you do dear? Play? The Church leadership is there to do what? *Do the work of ministry.* Halleluiah. The leaders are not responsible for the work of ministry. You are. It is your calling. *Uh, he is now deceiving us. What kind of a pastor is this one? Me I'm not called. I'm not called.* No wonder you are cold. Frozen Christian. **We have eternity to talk sweet things to each other. I'm not going to be nice to you now.** The work of God is in the pending tray because no one wants to do the delivery. *The pastor, the pastor. He is the one called.* Who told you that? God determined that you be born in this age for a **serious** reason. I hope the Darwin thing has not affected your thinking. **Things don't happen by chance**. There is a purpose. You are not called to be a Christian without a purpose.

Listen you are called or set for the defense of the gospel Philippians. 1:7. The word 'set' is not an accidental word. It means purpose, careful planning. Grand design. There is also wisdom. God set the great men and women of old to start the race, but at the back of His mind He knew you were going to finish the race in style.

In a 4 x 100 meter medley relay, your starter must be good. The ones in the middle should just maintain the position. But the finisher must be exceptional. You are the finisher. God has offered you such an opportunity don't mess it up, little child. You got all the backing and support from heaven. Look. God speaks big about you. He is always boasting. What are you doing now? **We are all looking towards you for victory.** Listen I do not know how you look at yourself. Probably your life and even your integrity has hit rock bottom. You are the kind Jesus needs. Come as you are and Jesus will change it all.

Many look to big names to do all the work of ministry. That is not God's design. You are overloading your friends. The labourers are few, how do you compound this problem by your laziness? You ought to do your part. Those big names can't do without you. **There are no parts of the body that are irrelevant.** You can't say I only need the legs I do not need my hands. Stop looking at yourself like a loser. You are family. We are the body. We need one another. The battle before us is not for big names, but for the body of Christ. You ,me and the others are the body. So who is a Christian?

Philippians 2:25

Epaphroditus was—

- Brother
- Worker
- **Soldier**
- Messenger
- Minister

The problem with the Church is that we just have brothers, sisters and ministers no soldiers. Sometimes I will rub you the other way so that I remove the dross. You are not supposed to be where you are. **I will take the pleasure of breaking that civilian mentality.** *Oh, this is hard, this* *is tough. Only great men and women can deal with it.* The pastor does not attend to trivial matters. Don't misuse power. To arrest an unruly drunk you don't call a battalion of super commandos. That's pure undiluted madness. Do you know what a commando is trained for? *But pastor Keyworth some things are hard. I may die.* Understood, you may die. Are you born again? *Yes.* Wonderful. Go well. Greetings to Paul and Silas. We'll meet later. **Church is not a day care.** Full of babies jostling for attention. That uniform of losers you are wearing, DROP IT! Judgment will be very severe for the Church leadership because we are producing weaklings, puppets and muppets that the Antichrist will recruit on his inauguration ceremony without any resistance.

It is now common knowledge the body of Christ thinks it has been called to 'pastor, pastor, pastor'. The body of Christ has been called to the work of ministry. You must do the work of ministry. Learn then teach others. Minister healing. Cast out devils. **The power gifts do not just work in pastors. That is one of the worst lies to ever come from hell.** The Bible tells the body of Christ (here God is not talking about pastors, prophets, teachers, evangelists. Apostles) no. The lay people must take up their positions. Eph. 4:15. The Word of God has power. But people take out this, take out that, and what remains? Thank you James. Tradition. And tradition does not scare the devil. For traditions are manufactured in his backyard. *Why do I seem hard?* Because while we are busy playing games, the devil has sent his special forces. We, I'm sorry to say this, unfortunately have been invaded. **The devil is in the Church.** The tares are in. Today there is abnormal **moneypulation** and manipulation. Why? Because some people are capitalizing on the ignorance of the saints. Church leadership is **moneypulating** and manipulating the saints, because they think the pastor or clergy is the body of Christ. Halleluiah.

They have crept in **unnoticed** Jude 4 tells us. We have been asleep, they entered undetected. Now the battle has to be fought from within. *But pastor we do not wrestle against flesh and blood, but against spiritual forces.* Thank you Tom, for educating us. We appreciate your wisdom. But know this. **God works through people. The devil works through people. It is common sense we must know both**.

Phil 3:17 *Join with others in following my example, brothers,*

and take note of those who live according to the pattern
we gave you. [18] *For, as I have often told you before*
and now say again even with tears, many live as
enemies of the cross of Christ. [19] *Their destiny*
is destruction, their god is their stomach,
and their glory is in their shame.
Their mind is on earthly
things. (NIV)

These commandos from the dark side are taking advantage of God's grace by indulging in sensual activities. Their desire is not Christ, but self–satisfaction. Pleasure, pleasure, pleasure. Demonic pleasure. I remember a discussion I had with a Doctor of Divinity about homosexuality. The Doc was direct, when he said, *'That is included in Geographical holiness'.* Being gay is included in Geo what? *Geographical holiness.* I went home educated. And like a good student I added a few. Mathematical, Chemical, Biological, Astronomical, Astrological and Mechanical Holinesses. **I'm now holier than ever before with all those 'icals'.** Listen I respect men and women of God. God Almighty is my real witness because He alone knows my deepest thoughts. Allow me to be a little bold and say : **God doesn't care what man calls you!** If you play around with God's Word, sending millions to hell, you will forever regret it. There have been people like you before, today they wish they could undo it all. Unfortunately it is too late. Never forget He alone, holds your heart in His palms, and when He decides it's time for it to cease beating, there is no reverse gear. You have thrown away all your life. **There is nothing as terrible as knowing you have missed God forever.** The punishment comes second to that in comparison. I know very well I ain't just bubbling.

Elise are you noticing the pattern? A lot of things are being accepted to soothe the demonic desires. Trying to create a balance at Jesus' expense? **Some genius says we do not need the Bible, but on the other hand we need witchcraft.** How do you substitute the Bible for some magic books? You want children in schools to read magic and not the Bible? *We don't need the Bible, it is segregative, but we can have books that teach magic. That way no one's rights will be trampled on.* Am I sensationalizing issues or is this a fact happening today? **Is this true or not?** Somebody answer me. They are doing it for their father, why can't we do a better job for Dad? Watch what the world is coming up with as solutions. And some of these things 'seem' to make sense. **There is nothing the devil comes up with that does not make sense to a defunct mind**.

Discern the spirit behind. Another issue. The world is facing a dangerous scourge: HIV/AIDS. How do we solve it? Yes Mr. Genius, what's your solution? *Legalize prostitution.* Since he is the most educated among us, let's clap for him. Clap, clap, clap. Fantastic idea. *Why didn't I think of it in the first place?* John, don't kill yourself for nothing. **It takes a rotten mind to come up with such putrefying ideas.** The standard in the Church is dropping, or is it the people who are dropping? Anyway, there is a dropping somewhere. We are conforming to the standard of the world. The word for 'world' actually means the 'times'. The Church is changing its standard according to the latest fashion. *Jesus, there is no great news like this one. We have become chameleons, I thought we were Christians.* 'Moderation,' they bellow. 'They all start with CH and end with NS'. When Moses mentioned that there was something wrong among the people, the first to attack him were the leaders. Moses was too serious to be of any good. Moderation was advocated for. **Well, shortly moderation killed them.**

V. Conclusion

Job 20:4 *Do you not know from of old, since the time*
that man was placed on the earth, 5 *That the*
triumphing of the wicked is short, and the
joy of the godless and defiled is
but for a moment?
(Amp)

A. Faith To Win 12

[1John 5:4] *For whatsoever is born of God overcometh the world: and this is the victory that overcometh the world, even our faith.*

Faith is the victory that overcomes the world and all the world can ever throw at us. It may sound strange but it is our key to success. Victory is a certainty. **The devil may fume, he may howl, he may even jump in the oven, his antics will not change the inevitable, our faith overcomes whatever he can throw at us.** The dragon has come on earth with a view to completely obliterating God's own. Anything that does not have his character must be destroyed. Convert or die.

And Satan has one great instrument, the man of sin, the man of lawlessness the Antichrist , his begotten. The first born among those headed for destruction. To fully grasp the beast, we must understand that the Beast is two–fold: **It is both an organization and a person. The organization has emerged before the person.** Jesus brought the Kingdom of God. Right? What did He say? The kingdom of God is in you. The saints though in the kingdom have the kingdom residing in them. What are we saying in English?

In a similar manner that the kingdom of God was in Jesus **when** He came the kingdom of Satan is in the Antichrist. The devil's kingdom is enshrined in this evil person. He is the very embodiment of Satan's beastly kingdom. The kingdom of God is righteousness peace and joy in the **HOLYSPIRIT**—our **Invisible Mark**.

The Antichrist is coming with solutions. But his solutions are only for those who bow before him. **All the food shortages you see are simple engineering problems from the pit of hell**. Don't fall for the lie. **Financial crunch? Economic crunch?** Please what's wrong with you? You have fallen for it? Read **'Satan's Best Kept Secrets'.** Here is a simple question: would you believe it if somebody told you that the financial crunch we saw was actually tabled in the *boardroom* over a hundred years ago? I don't think so. If ignorance was a subject at school nobody would fail it. We would all pass it with flying colors. Clap for yourself. What you are told and what they do are poles apart. Some people are even committing suicide because of the financial crunch. How can the world economy be your foundation? Come on Jesus must be. Don't build your life on quick sand. **Do you realize that the first group of people to be attacked in these last days are the workers?** Or best put bread winners? God knew a day would come when we would cry. We have just broken the record. We have gone beyond crying. **WE ARE SCREAMING!** We rejected Theocracy and brought in a substitute, Democracy. **Whatever you substitute for God's wisdom never works.** Why don't we learn? **If the Bible is right, the way that leads to life is narrow and the way that leads to destruction is wide then it is common sense the majority have made bad decisions. And if the majority have, then the majority do not desire the standard of God. If the majority do not desire God's standard then Democracy, which is a game of numbers (the majority) is a supersonic train to hell. The devil is taking over the world using democracy.** And he is doing it legally. Thanks to democracy! The devil's people are laughing. And we seem not to see it coming as Christians. Democracy will always work against God and His own. Some Christians have been shaking their heads in bitter disappointment. *How could our leaders legalize 'gays?'* Well, what is two plus one equal to? Correct fifty–nine! We put that to a vote? How many say fifty–nine? See? You lose pal. In democracy it is the numbers that count. Two plus one is what the masses want it to be, **not what it is!** In democracy there is nothing wrong with being 'gay'. Stop bothering them! It is part of democracy. **How can you attack innocent people and forget the real issue, the system?**

And the one who controls the system wins. The devil is happy. He really thinks we are fools. *I hope our behavior doesn't vindicate him.* Look at this for example. A few years ago, everyone was sure Communism was bad. Why? Communism was saying **There is no God**. It made all of us atheists. Democracy on the other hand in its final stages says **There is God**. Capital 'G.' Christians are jumping. Halleluiah. Democracy has actually turned us into believers in God. But it is not Jehovah, the Father of the Lord Jesus. **IT IS SATAN.** Believe it or not Satan today has more room, rights and audience than Jesus. Communism or Democracy? Now we are to choose between the lesser of two devils. What do you want, a poisoned apple or a poisoned sweet? Hmm. Sweet is appealing. But poison is poison. An option from the devil is never an option. We have been fooled. And if we don't open our eyes we are going to continue being fooled. **Whatever you substitute for God's wisdom never works.** We have so much confidence in our systems, if only we could have such confidence in God.

Hell's greatest asset is ignorance. People do not seem to want to know what is happening right before their eyes. Jesus told Nicodemus that if he could not understand the things that were happening on earth how would he understand those from heaven? It is the same today. The things that are being done we know, but like the good fellows we are we look the other side, to the devils enjoyment. Let's not hide the wickedness we are seeing. And never should we be intimidated. **The devil is under our feet so are all his puppies. We are not the kind that is intimidated. Fear does not run in us, but faith does.** When your sight is impaired you will be tossed to and fro. **Listen and listen very well, no one can kill you before your time, none.** It doesn't matter how desperate they are to get rid of you, they cannot kill you. Fear no one. **Fear nothing!**

The devil has no power over your life. And the best part he does not have the power of death either. Jesus destroyed him completely

Hebrews 2:14 *Forasmuch then as the children are partakers*
of flesh and blood, he also himself likewise took part
of the same; that through death he might destroy
him that had the power of death, that is,
the devil; 15 *And deliver them who*

through fear of death were
all their lifetime subject
to bondage.

Do not fear the devil and do not fear to die, you are bringing yourself under bondage. Don't go back to bondage, you have been released from it. Trust God to keep you. It is very shameful to note that most Christians are terrible cowards. They fear death very much to the extent that their talk is very different from their walk. **If your God is not worth dying for, either change yourself or change your God. Find someone worthy.** If your God is my God I know how the devil hates your presence. And he is at pains trying to deal with you. Good. Torture him. It's time we made him age because of pressure. He will look older than his age. You are not a civilian, but a commando. A super commando. Move aggressively in the name of Jesus! The only thing he can do is make you desperate to move out of God's safe hands using cooked up means like the economic down turn. When under pressure many become evil minded. They want to 'survive'. Families are sacrificing even their children just to get bread. Send them on the streets to sleep with anyone. Shame. The second beast targets bread winners mostly, why? Because once the bread winner or head of family is captured the rest follow suit. It is easy for a bread winner to persecute those under him. The idea is to get the leader and the rest will follow. Will you betray Jesus because of a morsel of bread? You have the birth right of the first born do not take it lightly. You will not have another opportunity again. Turn on your faith.

One cannot accept to let their newly born child to die when they can simply get the devil's mark and buy some formula for the child to feed, you say. Such psychological torture will be applied for you to recant. The words of the Bible ring deafeningly: **Here is the patience and faith of the saints.** Can you allow your family to starve to death just because you want to avoid the mark of the beast? Isn't that folly of the highest order? Yes it is folly. So? *Mark here I come.* And another soul goes into oblivion. Some people will be delivered miraculously, but others will have to face death. That is a time when evil *seems* to win. **But know that the devil never wins even when it seems so.** It appears so. But if you have studied, a real student of the Word you will know that the devil is a grand deceiver. **He is a failure through and through.**

He can never succeed. If you check in the spirit realm, it is totally a different matter. Yes that grave situation you are facing is not that grave in the spiritual realm. Satan is down under your feet. Romans 16:20. The devil is under. He is down. **If you are looking at the devil face to face then it is common sense you are upside down!!!**

Whatever happens hang in there do not recant. Do not capitulate. The Bible is clear when it says the shield of faith is the weapon by which you can **quench all** the fiery darts of the enemy. **All means all**. It means the worst onslaught to come your way can be overcome, by faith.

It does not matter when the military is sent after you. Oh by the way, there will be no wars that moment, the duty of the military and police is to hunt you down. Strange technology is being implemented even in the military at certain levels. The military is going to be a **grave instrument** to destroy many. All the technology you see is mostly designed with —you got that right—you in mind. **Believe it or not the new holocaust is here.** But that does not stop you and me. **That charges us**. The Word in us is like fire in our bones. Most of you still remember the tsunami, for it is something still etched on your minds. A few voices whispered that the tsunami was not a natural occurrence. It was manmade. Finger pointing became the name of the game. *'We told you it was a 'Fire Belt,' no nuclear experiments.'* Do you remember that? You do. **This is the problem today, what we know we force ourselves not to know**. What followed? Policies. Policies were to be implemented that would make the world more secure. In English they were saying they needed a grip so that none of us is really free. A supervisor or captain of the world had to be found. Someone has to monitor all of us. I do not know whether the tsunami was a natural catastrophe or it was 'manufactured'. But I know that some issues that followed point to one thing: **World security under one world police.** *It may not be strange to infer that some things that happen are done so that there is justification for the steps some of our policy makers take.* But no matter the situation, world police, wild police or wild policy we move on with the flaming Gospel of Jesus. Undeterred. It is very true that some of the policies being enacted or passed are shocking. These policies one can see through them all the way from planet X. I repeat it is not every throne (government) that is of God. The Bible is clear.

Psalm 94:20 *Shall the throne of iniquity have fellowship with thee, which frameth mischief by a law?*

Have you seen that? **This seat of sin makes evil into law.** That is a complex issue if you are a Christian. You are told to obey those who rule over you, but they are pouring demonic laws, how can we follow that? The Christian is confused. Don't be confused dear. **Welcome to middle Basic school! The devil's ultimate goal in democracy is to make government not function under divine authority but as divine authority!** If you do good you are going against the law. How many Christians have suffered because they came strongly against sin? Witchcraft today is okay. Abortion is being encouraged not because of the reasons they give us, but because of the ones they hold back. Some industries are making a lot from the buying of foetuses from unsuspecting victims. Homosexuality is not sin, it is a fashion. *My heart sincerely goes to my dear beloved ones who have found themselves trapped in homosexuality. Some truly believe they were born that way. Others for the sake of the economy they are trapped. My heart bleeds for them. They genuinely do not know how some people who are directly in contact with the spirit world are unleashing spells on them. Please careful how we handle homosexuals or gays. There are two groups, those who know what they are doing and those who don't. Don't you dare throw the baby with the water!* If anyone says anything on the contrary or to the contrary the law will visit him. And what is so interesting is the way truth is being covered. Allow a little to trickle but bury the whole ice berg. We have seen a rise in 'experts.' Who '*experted*' them only the devil can tell. These experts refute the truth and introduce lies to calm the masses. That could only mean two things

- The experts have themselves been fooled. The expert has been deceived by his superiors. Complex life, huh?

2Timothy 3:12 *In fact, everyone who wants to live a godly life in Christ Jesus will be persecuted,* 13 *while evil men and impostors will go from bad to worse, deceiving and being deceived.*

- The experts are being used by an **invisible hand**

> Isaiah 59:15 *Yes, truth is lacking, and he who departs from evil makes himself a prey. And the Lord saw it, and it displeased Him that there was no justice.*

If you dare leave the position of supporting sin, you become a target. Secret societies have formed a great coalition and have devised ways of trapping many on a global scale. They are using four factors to enlist people.

> 1John 2:16 *For all that is in the world, the lust of the flesh, and the lust of the eyes, and the pride of life, is not of the Father, but is of the world.*

Seen them?

- **The lust of the flesh**
- **The lust of the eyes, and**
- **The pride of life**

But the major reason people are going for the devil without reservation is clear, they **love him and enjoy what he stands for.** It is clear undiluted rebellion. That is why it is called Lawlessness. They want to be governed by the devil not God. Our society has one thing and one thing only, support evil or perish. Our society is morally gone, finished, interred. Sin is the latest trend, if you do not sin you are old fashioned. Truly the mark is being given at alarming levels and many have received it. You do not need to be a Bible scholar to check your life and be sober. What is happening around us must be enough to let us see the truth of the Bible and repent seriously. Is this true or is the Bible just crazy? It is no secret, the truth is what the Bible declares. Many would want us not to speak out. Speaking we will. The Lord has sent us and the Word in us is flaming hot.

> Jeremiah 20:9 *But if I say, "I will not mention him or speak*

any more in his name," his word is in my heart
like a fire, a fire shut up in my bones.
I am weary of holding it in;
indeed, I cannot.

We cannot keep quiet even if we wanted to! Yes those who were saved by the crosses on the sides will keep quiet. For there were three crosses on Golgotha that day. I cannot know which one they bowed to. But you and me recognize only one cross, the one in the middle. And that cross in the middle makes us fearless. Nothing will catch us by surprise. **We are not getting ready we live ready.**

Never bow before your enemy. It's not humility. It's madness. **Humility is your position in God not your posture before the devil.** I am not entering Heaven using the back door as a sissy, no, never. **I am entering Heaven as a general and Jesus giving me a standing ovation, what about you?** What is your idea? Back door? Don't you dare think about that. You are not a sissy. **You are not a sissy.** Let the power in you arise. The power of God is upon you. The anointing to do the impossible runs in your life. Don't you ever run from your enemy. Let me leave you with a scripture that made me nearly drop my jaw the first time I saw it. How God does not compromise on courage.

Jeremiah 1:17 *But you(put your name), gird up your loins! Arise*
and tell them all that I command you. Do not be
dismayed and break down at the sight of
their faces, lest I confound you before
them and permit you to
be overcome.
(brackets mine)

God is saying if you cower before your enemies, I will embarrass you before them. **Courage in God's kingdom is not optional.** Courage is not optional. Courage is your nature. And know that the anointing you carry works in the presence of courage. **Without courage the anointing does not work.** Fear? Never fear. Speak boldly. Live aloud. If you don't, God Himself will embarrass you before your enemies. I am confident you are the person the Lord Jesus is proud to call His own. His firebrand. May His flaming message burn in you and may you deliver it as He wants it. Saint, it does not matter how the **Enemy** play it. We have the **Official Results: WE HAVE WON!!!**

PRAYER OF SALVATION

If you would like to know Jesus as your Saviour and Lord, don't miss the moment.

PRAY THIS PRAYER.

God I come to you
in the name of Jesus.
Lord I confess my
sins and I ask your
son Jesus to
come into my life. Let Him be Lord and Saviour of my life. I forsake the kind of life I have been leading and let the Holy Spirit come into
my life. I recognize the blood
of Jesus that was shed
for me. I thank you
God for hearing me
I thank you Jesus
for coming to
live in me and
with me.
Amen.

For any spiritual help, contact us and we will be more than glad to be of help.

2010 RELEASES BY PASTOR KEYWORTH N. NGOSA

(Soon to be released)

SATAN'S BEST KEPT SECRETS

ABIDE: THE KEY TO FREEDOM

PETER'S REVELATION

MASTERS OF DREAMS

THE MIRACLE OF DEATH AND BIRTH